KATIE'S STORY

Let God's Light Shine In Me

Sarah J. Cobb and Katie Cobb

35th Star Publishing
www.35thstar.com
Charleston, West Virginia

ISBN-13: 978-1-7350739-0-3
ISBN-10: 1-7350739-0-3

RELIGION / Christian Living / Inspirational
RELIGION / Christian Living / Personal Memoirs

35th Star Publishing
www.35thstar.com
Charleston, West Virginia

Cover design and interior layout: Studio 6 Sense LLC • studio6sense.com

#LetGodsLightShineInMe

Katie

Dedicated to
Kate Elizabeth Cobb
8/28/2003 - 10/10/2017

I can hardly wait to see your smile,
hear your laugh,
and hug your neck.

I'll see you soon, girl.

Foreword

God told me. In the most audible words I have ever heard from him, he told me. Katie was in the hospital with a chest tube and an impending cancer diagnosis. My husband, Chad, had spent the night there with her so I could sleep at home with our other kids. I awoke that morning holding my chest, as if my heart was being torn apart and I was trying to hold it together with my bare hands. I sat on my couch, rocking back and forth, simply saying, "Jesus… Jesus," over and over again. As I struggled to climb the steps to awaken my children for school, I cried big tears and said repeatedly, "You can't take her from me! I love her! I need her!" In that moment, God dropped me to my knees. I paused there, sobbing, as I heard him say, "Shhhh. This is not about you. This is Katie's story."

This is Katie's story.

The story of who she was and who she became. It is the story of childhood cancer and some of the atrocities it brings. It is the story of suffering and bravery. Fear and courage. It is the story of Katie's pursuit of God and his pursuit of her.

Katie's story unfolds from two perspectives. Sarah's (mine) and Katie's. I share my perspective in vignettes. These short scenes, snippets of time and emotion, enable you to know this child in a way that goes beyond simply knowing about her. They share small parts of her life, her struggles, her personality and even her death. My perspective tells the true story of Katie. Katie's perspective is taken directly from her own writings and journals, including her quiet times, sermon notes, Bible studies and blog posts. They are her exact words, just as she wrote them, captured in a font uniquely inspired by her own handwriting. Although Katie's writings are not in exact chronological order, she wrote most of the journals in the first two parts of the book before she was diagnosed with cancer. The majority of the entries in the latter two parts were written throughout the course of her illness, right up to the week before her death. Katie's perspective tells the story of her relationship with God and her desire to reflect His light through her life. Collectively, they are the book we wrote together, although not the story we dreamed of telling.

Katie's life. God's light.

This is Katie's story.

Acknowledgments

When my kids were all little hand-holders visiting the library with me, I often related to the children's librarian that one of my crazy goals in life was to write a children's book. I quipped, "… because my life is full of stories that are just as good as any of these." I intended to eventually go back through my memories and my journals, digging out a fun family shenanigan to adapt into a children's story. That is the way I dreamed of writing a book and, as it turns out, that is exactly what I did. But I never dreamed of writing this book.

I am so grateful that Laura Boggess, my friend and mentor, dreamed some of it for me. After a few seasons apart, God led her back into my life just as I began to record my memories of Katie. She aptly advised me to "just write the stories and God will put it together." You were so right, Laura. Thank you for believing in the power of words to bring healing and for binding up some of my wounds along the way.

Bob and Sarah Akers, your presence in our life is a blessing beyond expression. Thank you for sitting in the pit of grief with us day in and day out. Thank you for reading my first draft of muddled writings and offering the shape it needed to grow. Thank you for corrections, suggestions, and lots of encouragement. Thank you for a key and open invitation to your sacred writing space. And Bob, thank you for poring through Katie's journals, finding each letter and distinct character, and then crafting a font that mimics her handwriting so beautifully. I wept when I saw the final creation, and I have no doubt you wept as you created it.

Thanks to the special people who helped mold my manuscript into a bona fide book. To MaryBeth, Monica and Carly, I appreciate your willingness to read through various versions of the story and offer feedback. Thessa, thank you for lovingly and painfully helping to caption each photo in a way that reflects Katie. To Liz Giertz, thank you for editing with honesty and tenderness. I am happy to have found another writer friend in you. To Steve Cunningham and the team at 35th Star Publishing, thank you for your excitement in publishing Katie's Story. I am grateful that you allowed it to be what I envisioned but with more beauty than I thought possible. Special thanks to Jason Hager for helping me to promote a story more than a person.

Thank you to the team of physicians, nurses and ancillary staff who cared for Katie in Charleston, West Virginia, and in Cincinnati, Ohio. We are deeply grateful for your brilliant minds and compassionate hearts which enable you to fight the brokenness of this world every day. Special thanks to Elizabeth Young, Ashley Meyer, Robin Norris, Priscila Badia, Benjamin Mizukawa, Molly Haskell, Katie Bradford and Chevy. You have touched our lives in ways we never expected and ways we will never forget.

To our family and friends who are too many in number to name. Thank you for all the ways you loved on us during the time of Katie's illness and long after her death. We are deeply aware of so many things you did for us and likely completely unaware of many others. We cannot thank you enough for your role in meeting our most basic needs.

To all of Katie's friends. Thank you for allowing me to share your stories. And thank you for allowing me to remain a part of your lives. We need each other. In many ways, I connect you to your sweet friend and you connect me to my daughter. While you will not have opportunities to create new memories with Katie, I hope you will go on to live and enjoy life on earth. Please tell me about it! Send me pictures and stories. I want to celebrate and cry and encourage you just as Katie would have. Sure, I might shed a tear or twenty, but I am still very, very happy for you.

To my children: Aaron, Katie, Ben, Annie and Daniel. You are such fun people with great personalities, and I truly enjoy you. You teach me way more than I teach you. You make me better in so many ways. Thank you for believing I can do anything. I am blessed to have been chosen as your mom, and I am enormously grateful for every single day I get to spend with you.

To Chad, my love. We experienced the unthinkable. And it was just as bad as we could have imagined. Yet while we were at our weakest, we found a strength we didn't know existed. We faced Katie's death together. And we healed together. We are so much better together than we are alone. Thank you for encouraging me to write Katie's Story - even if only for us. Our kids may believe I can do anything, but you are the one who enables it.

Jesus. Thank you for letting me pound your chest with my fists. Thank you for sitting with me when I had nothing to say to you. Thank you for not leaving me alone in the darkness. Thank you for speaking to my heart so clearly that I could not deny it. And thank you for using the deepest pain in my life to produce a hope and longing for you that will never disappoint.

Table of Contents

Introduction

Meet Katie

Katie had not yet grown into her name when she died at the age of 14. We wanted a daughter named Katie, but we wanted her to also have a grown-up name. Our preference was not toward Katelyn or Katherine or the many variations thereof, so we simply named her Kate. We always told her, "One day, when you become an adult, you can be Kate. If you want. But you'll always be Katie to us." Of course, others mimicked her parents. We called her Katie, her teachers called her Katie, her friends called her Katie. As she moved into the tween and teen years and began experimenting with finding her identity through fashion trends and hair styles, she easily could have moved to Kate. She certainly didn't mind when someone called her Kate, but the signature she created, the personality she exhibited, and the story she composed with her life was Katie.

She wrote about herself:

I am a very outgoing person and always love to pass a smile on to someone else! Also, I feel that I am a good leader and am a very caring person. I am organized and disciplined. As well as, a good rapport with my teachers. I am a friendly person that loves to see others succeed!

I have faced the challenge of feeling not good enough or being different from others. However, I have learned that it's okay to be different! Be a leader and not a follower! When I have problems with friends, I try to use as much patience as I can and calmly talk it through with them. I live life based on what Jesus thinks of me and not others.

Katie was affectionate, joyful, compassionate, gracious, disciplined. Her spirit was so determined. Her spunk so enjoyable. She coated her sassiness with love in such a way that you hardly noticed it. Her smile, so beautiful and contagious that no one ever forgot it. Her life was such that only God could have crafted it.

Meet Sarah

I grew up in the hills of West Virginia amid a small community and a large family. It was there I was introduced to Jesus as a child and grew up in a Christian family that never missed a church service. However, it was not until my young adult years that I began to pursue a deeper relationship with God, one that extended beyond Sunday mornings and into my everyday life.

When a friend introduced Chad and I in college, we immediately knew our relationship would lead to marriage. For the first ten years of our life together, I worked as a nurse in the emergency room at a local hospital while Chad designed roads and water systems as a civil engineer. Through an interesting turn of events, Chad and I made the decision that he should change his career path to ministry.

Somewhere along our way together, I submitted not only to motherhood but also to mothering a large family—at least by current standards. The first four (Aaron, Kate, Benjamin, and Anne) were born in less than seven years. Daniel, our fifth child, was born a few years behind the rest. We prayed for Daniel and fought through the agony of a miscarriage to have him. He was born in the middle of my graduate courses as I pursued my degree and certification as a nurse practitioner. Daniel brought our young family together in an incredible way, adding just the right touch of completion.

In 2016, River Ridge Church was thriving under Chad's leadership. I was working part-time in the emergency room as a nurse practitioner and full-time as chief of operations in our home. Aaron and Katie were young teenagers, starting to think about driving and honors courses and spending more time with their friends. Ben and Annie were in elementary school, trying out music and sports and growing into their own unique personalities. And Daniel, our caboose, was all giggles and dimples and dinosaur pajamas. Life was good. And life was pretty easy.

Several years prior, while discipling a small group of twenty-something women, we had a discussion about preparing for the storms of life. I had told them... *when life is easy and the skies are clear, that's when you grab onto the belief that God is good. Not in the way that you and I define good, but in the way that he defines good. You study that and learn that and get your arms all the way around that because the storm is coming. It's coming. And when the wind blows and the rain pours and the hail pounds you in the face, you better hope that you can just barely keep your fingernails in your belief that God is good. But you better get your arms around your faith now when you can still see it.*

That's what I told them. Then the wind started to pick up.

PART 1

Before Cancer

Katie

Be still in the light of God's presence.

Sarah

Born on August 28, 2003, only 19 months behind her brother, Katie was quite the pleasant surprise. As an infant, I remember holding her and saying, "Oh, Katie. You're probably going to be a girly girl, and I don't know anything about fixing hair or painting nails or doing makeup. I hope you'll be patient with me. Maybe one day you'll teach me." And she did. That girl taught me so many things.

For years, she had thin, dirty blond hair which hardly grew at all. As it began to darken and slowly gain a bit of length, she experimented with braids, practicing on me as I sat on the floor and she sat on the couch behind me. "Would you let me dye my hair with Kool-Aid?" she asked around sixth grade. "Ummm, sure," I shrugged, "it's just hair." There are certainly worse things to worry about. So, we mixed the packets of Kool-Aid and hot water, started the timer and watched the red or blue dye creep onto the ends of her hair. She loved the color and the fun it added to her summer. Little did I know that her hair had a tendency to hold on to that color for a long time, and the blue or red tips remained for months after.

It was around this same time of her life that she began to fall in love. Somewhere around age 11, while Katie was enamored with painted toenails, sunshine and how to take a cute selfie, God began wooing her. He was pursuing her, drawing her to himself. She began journaling. Not as in "Dear Diary, the boy in my math class is cute." Not as in "My mom drives me crazy because she won't let me get a phone." No, these were journals comprised of her thoughts about God and his words to her. Scriptures and questions and take away points from studies and teachings and Bible passages. She didn't write about boys and frustrations and outfits and arguments. She wrote about her faith.

She began to look for God to show up, and she began to listen for his voice. She knew it was him. I didn't tell her. Her daddy didn't tell her. But she knew.

God's voice is something we train ourselves to hear. We learn it during the quiet times, as we read his Word, converse with him through prayer and pay attention to what happens next. Once we know his voice, we can hear it more easily. We can identify it above the cacophony of life. I often compare it to a mother and her baby. That mother spends time with her child, holding and consoling. In the quiet of her house, she hears him clearly when he cries for his next feeding or diaper change. A momma knows that sweet cry—the voice of a baby intended specifically for her ears. So, the next time she lets a friend hold her child in a crowded room with people chattering, kids laughing and infants squalling, she will hear that one cry across the room, and she will say, "Excuse me, that's my baby crying." *Because she knows.* She knows that voice. She has spent hours and hours listening to it in the quiet. What others miss because of the noise, she hears because she is attuned to it. So it is with the voice of God. We recognize it in the chaos because we have learned it in the calm.

And during this quiet season, Katie was tuning her ears. She was learning to be still in God's presence. He was infusing his light into her little body. He was already teaching her to live above her circumstances and filling her with joy no one could take away.

Fortunately, she didn't trade her painted toenails or Kool-Aid dyed hair for this growing relationship with God. She just took them with her.

◁

Katie

I should constantly be seeking God.

I'm really only beginning my journey of intimacy with God.

It's not an easy road, but it's a delightful & privileged way—like a treasure hunt.

God is the treasure!

Hardships are part of the journey too!

Trust God & don't be afraid.

Psalm 27:8

2 Corinthians 5:7

Isaiah 12:2

My heart says of you, "Seek his face!"

— Psalm 27:8

For we live by faith, not by sight.

— 2 Corinthians 5:7

Surely God is my salvation;
I will trust and not be afraid.
The Lord, the Lord himself, is my strength and my defense;
he has become my salvation.

— Isaiah 12:2

Sarah

Katie met Jesus when she was very young. Sure, we talked about God on Sunday, but it was Monday to Saturday when we lived it. Even at that, Katie's big brother, Aaron, was the one who really introduced her to Jesus. Aaron prayed with Katie. Katie prayed with Ben. I witnessed my children's confidence as they approached God, passing down their faith in a way that humbled me. Katie was baptized at age seven by her daddy. I can imagine no greater experience than to receive your children into your earthly family and then to baptize them into your heavenly family, confirming that you will truly love and enjoy them for all eternity.

Katie's earliest journals came from her times at church camp, when she feverishly wrote notes from the chapel services and pondered questions about her faith. She came home from camp excited about stronger relationships with the friends who accompanied her and new friendships with the girls she met during the week. The new friendships that stayed the course, however, were often the counselors. She was drawn to those who were slightly older, slightly more mature and slightly more interested in Jesus than horseback riding and swimming. Unbeknownst to me, Katie sent birthday messages to those girls and checked in with them throughout the year. She was very good at pursuing people;.

The camp experiences, the early journaling and the friendships were all integral to the initial stages of her intimate relationship with Jesus. She began to fall in love with him, to desire him outside of Sunday morning, to put in the time necessary to truly know him. Intimacy comes only with time and attention and, somehow, she knew that. Sure, we encourage our kids to spend time reading their Bibles and we model for them how to pray, but lots of people work their religious habits without really attending to the relationship. We teach and model in hopes that the desire follows the habit, eventually driving the habit. With Katie, it did. She once told her friend Maddie, "You just have to do it, Maddie. Just make yourself get up and read your Bible and then you'll love it and you'll just want to!"

Katie was not deterred in her faith simply because she was young. She was learning to seek God in the day to day, recognizing that intimacy with him was the goal— the treasure—even though the search for it would not always be easy.

◁

Katie

1 Corinthians 12:18-27

Whatever you are asked to do, do it with all your might.

We are not more or less important than anyone else. The most important role is the one you are asked to play. Play your heart out!!

Ephesians 3:7-11

I am a runner, a student, and a follower of Christ. Sometimes I feel like I'm not needed, but my role wouldn't exist if I wasn't needed.

Do your best @ everything you do. You're always needed!

But in fact God has placed the parts in the body, every one of them, just as he wanted them to be. If they were all one part, where would the body be? As it is, there are many parts, but one body. The eye cannot say to the hand, "I don't need you!" And the head cannot say to the feet, "I don't need you!" On the contrary, those parts of the body that seem to be weaker are indispensable, and the parts that we think are less honorable we treat with special honor. And the parts that are unpresentable are treated with special modesty, while our presentable parts need no special treatment. But God has put the body together, giving greater honor to the parts that lacked it, so that there should be no division in the body, but that its parts should have equal concern for each other. If one part suffers, every part suffers with it; if one part is honored, every part rejoices with it. Now you are the body of Christ, and each one of you is a part of it.

— 1 Corinthians 12:18-27

I now serve the good news because God gave me his grace. His power is at work in me. I am by far the least important of all the Lord's holy people. But he gave me the grace to preach to the Gentiles about the unlimited riches that Christ gives. God told me to make clear to everyone how the mystery came about. In times past it was kept hidden in the mind of God, who created all things. He wanted the rulers and authorities in the heavenly world to come to know his great wisdom. The church would make it known to them. That was God's plan from the beginning. He has fulfilled his plan through Christ Jesus our Lord.

— - Ephesians 3:7-11 (NIrV)

Sarah

I find it harder to send my kids to middle school than to kindergarten. Something about middle school feels like a minefield where good kids can explode into poor choices without any warning. Perhaps it is my own memories of that age tainting my anticipation of it or perhaps it is the next layer of control that drops from my grip as they step into that season of life. Middle school is hard for both kids and mommas. Yet, somehow, my oldest kids grew stronger, made more friends, became more disciplined during those years. Not weaker, fewer, less.

Katie decided to venture into sports in middle school. She had played some soccer at the YMCA through the years but nothing more. Organized track was a first for her, with expectations of regular runs, personal records and pushing herself beyond what was easy or comfortable. She thought she wanted to sprint, but her small stature and short legs were a limiting factor in that arena. Longer distances seemed to suit her better. She was never the fastest, but she worked hard and did not quit. The following year she tried cross country. She loved being on the team and encouraging others. She was disciplined enough to train hard but not so focused that she neglected the people around her.

With five kids in various activities and my work requiring a couple evening shifts each week, Katie often had to ride with other families to practices and meets. I think she convinced every parent with whom she rode to stop for milkshakes afterward! Katie liked to run hard, but she liked to eat sweets and laugh even more. Although I may regret the occasions that I missed seeing her run, her friends and their parents share with me how much they appreciated those opportunities to enjoy her company.

Sometimes when I took her to cross country practice, she invited me to run hill sprints with the team. Seriously, how many middle school kids want their moms to run hill sprints with them and their friends? Perhaps she hoped I would fall and embarrass myself, but still I joined her and the team running up that grassy hill then huffing and puffing on the way down. It was always fantastic to be a part of her enthusiasm.

The next track season, Katie decided to learn to pole vault. At four feet and eleven inches tall, I don't know exactly what prompted her to begin learning this completely new and challenging sport. Nevertheless, she was buoyed by her friend,

Dianna, who was seven inches taller and had been practicing the technique for years. The truth is, Katie was not really very good at it. At first, she could barely run with the pole in her hand. Often, she did not even clear the bar. More than once, during a meet, when she was so upset about not succeeding, her friends rallied around to cheer and lift her spirits. Katie had often been the giver of encouragement, and this was her turn to be the recipient. She was thrilled when she finally succeeded in vaulting over the bar and achieving a personal record! Although her score did not earn any points in the meet, it was an achievement all her own. Katie, however, was not driven by superlatives. She did not work hard to be the fastest in the heat, the smartest in the class or first at anything. Katie's desire to be the best version of herself is what ignited her discipline.

She did the same thing when she opted to try volleyball during her eighth-grade year. With no prior volleyball experience other than hitting with friends in the backyard, she committed to learning the game. She was thrilled to make the team and even earned some varsity playing time. She loved the camaraderie with those girls and the encouragement from her coaches. I think Katie received the "Heart and Hustle" award at every sports banquet she ever attended.

In her off seasons, Katie did her own workouts. She found a blog called *blogilates* which gave a workout plan for each day that consisted of short videos of various exercises. She printed the workout calendar to hang on her wall and unfailingly completed her planks and lunges, often inviting or challenging me to do them with her. She talked and smiled about the girl named Cassey who ran the blog, as if she was just another of her many friends.

On whatever team she participated and in whatever role she played, Katie always did her best. She did not perceive herself as worse or better than anyone else, but she always played her heart out. She worked hard from every position in her life because she saw that as a component of bringing God's light to those around her.

◁

Katie

God doesn't just use special people. He takes random people and uses them in extraordinary ways.

1 Corinthians 1:27

Moses and the burning bush. God knew all about his stuttering but still asked him to do it.

Gideon is asked to lead but thinks he's too weak.

King David

God wants others to see Him in you, not your brokenness.

Peter denied God, but then God asks him to take care of His people.

The greatest ability is availability.

Rely on God. We can't do it on our own!

> But God chose the foolish things of the world to shame the wise; God chose the weak things of the world to shame the strong.
> — 1 Corinthians 1:27

Sarah

Katie did not stand out as a special kid by most cultural standards. She was rather small in stature and the youngest in her class with a late August birthday. She was not a stellar athlete or a remarkable musician. She was not the best dressed or the most popular in her class. But Katie was willing to seek out new endeavors, to gain new knowledge and to pursue new opportunities. She was unassuming to others, yet Katie assumed God could still use her to be and do something incredible.

Learning almost always came easy for Katie. She was an avid reader and loved math. Science was her least favorite subject, although she certainly held her own in that area as well. In fifth grade, she earned a spot in the school spelling bee. I am certain she told me, but she never made a big deal about it. So, for some reason, I did not make any effort to attend. When Katie and the principal called to tell me she had won, I was so excited for her and yet so ashamed I had not been present for her victory.

The following year, when she earned a spot in the middle school spelling bee, I was not about to miss it. I took my squirmy toddler with me, thinking we could slip out after she misspelled in the early rounds. After all, she was a sixth grader in this school of over 600 students. Thankfully, one of the teachers offered to occupy Daniel while I sat mesmerized in my chair, watching her go tet-a-tet with an eighth-grade boy for several rounds until she finally misspelled some four-syllable word. A word I had likely mispronounced when she was studying her stack of notecards several inches thick. She was so determined. She may have looked small, but she was fierce. She may have looked weak, but she was strong.

In seventh grade, Katie was the speller to beat. The previous champion had moved on to high school. I was going to get it right this time. I left work early to be there. I found a seat near the front row of parents. I did not take the toddler. She lived up to everyone's expectations and spelled like a champ—becoming the champ. It was so nerve-wracking and yet exhilarating to be present for her. Isn't that such a parallel of life with our kids? Nerve-wracking yet exhilarating. Scary yet thrilling. Daunting yet glorious.

Katie went on to the Putnam County Spelling Bee that year, but she did not stay up for the final round. She was okay with that. She said she never really wanted to go on to the regional bee, anyhow. She did not care that much about winning, but she couldn't *not* try. Once again, she competed against herself not others. People were too valuable for her to ever consider a trophy to be worth having an adversary.

During her eighth-grade year, when she would have again been the favored speller, she was at home, having just finished her first round of chemotherapy. That year, she cheered from afar for the participants in the Winfield Middle School Spelling Bee, which they conducted in honor of this little, humble girl with the big heart.

◁

Katie

Relationships. We should form deep, authentic relationships. The apostle Paul showed this.

Proverbs 27:17, Hebrews 10:23-25, Romans 1:11-12.

Friendships should be encouraging.

VULNERABILITY. Giving somebody the power to hurt you but trusting they won't. Evidence of solid friendship between 2 people. What it takes to build a deep, authentic friendship.

Phil 2:3-5. ✱ Building deep, authentic relationships. ✱ We can learn to care for other people. ✱ I am less, you are more. ✱ Not your own interests, but the interests of others. ✱ That's what God did.

Challenge - be a part of something that is bigger than yourself!!

As iron sharpens iron, so one person sharpens another.

— Proverbs 27:1

Let us hold unswervingly to the hope we profess, for he who promised is faithful. And let us consider how we may spur one another on toward love and good deeds, not giving up meeting together, as some are in the habit of doing, but encouraging one another—and all the more as you see the Day approaching.

— Hebrews 10:23-25

I long to see you so that I may impart to you some spiritual gift to make you strong–that is, that you and I may be mutually encouraged by each other's faith.

— Romans 1:11-12

Do nothing out of selfish ambition or vain conceit. Rather, in humility value others above yourselves, not looking to your own interests but each of you to the interests of the others. In your relationships with one another, have the same mindset as Christ Jesus.

— Philippians 2:3-5

Sarah

Katie and I had occasional conversations about school and different school options. In addition to friends at her own school, she had friends from other surrounding schools as well as friends who were home schooled. She had school friends, church friends and other friends, and she had no issue with what school option they chose. Katie, however, loved attending school. She was a true extrovert and enjoyed the socialization as much as the academics. As we talked on one particular day, she spoke about the other kids in her school, saying, "I love those people! I don't even know them all, but I need them!"

We often called Katie our social butterfly. She engaged so many different groups of people—perhaps in different ways and for different purposes—but she enjoyed them all. She had remained close with several friends since elementary school and two in particular—Maddie and Ella—had been her faithful friends since before any of them could remember. She had her volleyball friends and her track friends. She had friends from church, from the neighborhood and from classes at school. She had cousins she called friends even when she did not see them as often as others. She had friends from camp several years ago. She had older friends—twenty-somethings who took her out for lunch and pedicures. And she had younger friends—elementary and preschool-age kids who loved to receive her attention. She had so many close friends that Aaron made fun of her for it. "How many best friends can you have?" he often asked.

She kept track of all their birthdays and loved to give gifts on holidays, often spending so much of her own money that I discouraged using all of her saved money on gifts. We tried to come up with other ways to celebrate all these friends without breaking the bank. One year I helped her make little stockings to fill with candy. Another year she had a Christmas party instead of giving gifts. She wrote notes—sweet, handwritten notes of encouragement to teachers and friends—often accompanied by a homemade muffin or cookie.

Katie loved relationships. Deep, authentic relationships. She considered the interests of others, regardless of who they were or how well she knew them, but she also sought out those girls and women who could be mutually encouraging to her. She created space for a plethora of friendships in her life, but she especially pursued those that allowed for vulnerability and the sharpening of one another.

Katie

2 Corinthians 3:2-3

Just like a bike when you slam the brakes on, leave a mark to show where you've been. But instead of making black like a tire, make it look as much like Christ as possible.

Influence others for Christ.

Sometimes, my mark resembles Christ.

Today, I could leave my mark by being really nice, loving, caring, giving and all-around selfless.

John 4:39

1 Corinthians 2:1-5

Philippians 1:12-13

You yourselves are our letter, written on our hearts, known and read by everyone. You show that you are a letter from Christ, the result of our ministry, written not with ink but with the Spirit of the living God, not on tablets of stone but on tablets of human hearts.

— 2 Corinthians 3:2-3

Many of the Samaritans from that town believed in him because of the woman's testimony…

— John 4:39

And so it was with me, brothers and sisters. When I came to you, I did not come with eloquence or human wisdom as I proclaimed to you the testimony about God.

For I resolved to know nothing while I was with you except Jesus Christ and him crucified. I came to you in weakness with great fear and trembling. My message and my preaching were not with wise and persuasive words, but with a demonstration of the Spirit's power, so that your faith might not rest on human wisdom, but on God's power.

— 1 Corinthians 2:1-5

Now I want you to know, brothers and sisters, that what has happened to me has actually served to advance the gospel. As a result, it has become clear throughout the whole palace guard and to everyone else that I am in chains for Christ.

— Philippians 1:12-13

Sarah

In middle school, Katie started getting up early before school so that she could read her Bible, do some exercises and take her time getting ready for the day. She often woke up before me and was sitting on the couch with God when I stumbled through the family room to start the morning rush. Breakfast food at our house on school days is generally something super quick and easy. With a family of seven, that's just the way it is. Katie did not like protein shakes or cereal or frozen sausage links, but, man, that girl loved carbs! She decided she wanted a "real breakfast," as she called it (read: carb-laden, homemade yumminess), so she set her alarm to 5:30 a.m. on Tuesday mornings. Every Tuesday, she woke up extra early to start her routine and, by the time the rest of the house was stirring, Katie had Belgian waffles or homemade biscuits waiting for us.

You can leave a mark for Christ anywhere you are, but Tuesday mornings were the day Katie left her mark on breakfast. Although not entirely selfless, everyone in our house appreciated this little act of love that resembled Christ in a modern, teenage-girl kind of way.

◁

Katie

Facing Temptations

Shut the door on people pleasing.

"Why fit in when you were born to stand out?" - Dr. Seuss

You can't do anything about peer pressure, but you can do something about people pleasing. You don't have to please anybody. You just have to please God. Live and love like Jesus lived and loved.

Daniel 1

People pleasing mixes up what I think, say, and do. It starts with peer pressure. Daniel was pressured by: change in where he lived (v. 3), knew others liked what they saw (v. 4), they invested in him (v. 5), changed his name (v. 7), fear/respect of people (v. 9).

Daniel shut the door on people pleasing by thinking: "I will please God over pleasing people."

Daniel shut the door on people pleasing by saying/doing: Find my identity in Christ (my catch phrase)

Expect your faith to be tested.

The benefit of pleasing God is... the blessing (v. 17-21).

Then the king ordered Ashpenaz, chief of his court officials, to bring into the king's service some of the Israelites from the royal family and the nobility— young men without any physical defect, handsome, showing aptitude for every kind of learning, well informed, quick to understand, and qualified to serve in the king's palace. He was to teach them the language and literature of the Babylonians. The king assigned them a daily amount of food and wine from the king's table. They were to be trained for three years, and after that they were to enter the king's service. Among those who were chosen were some from Judah: Daniel, Hananiah, Mishael and Azariah. The chief official gave them new names: to Daniel, the name Belteshazzar; to Hananiah, Shadrach; to Mishael, Meshach; and to Azariah, Abednego. But Daniel resolved not to defile himself with the royal food and wine, and he asked the chief official for permission not to defile himself this way. Now God had caused the official to show favor and compassion to Daniel.

To these four young men God gave knowledge and understanding of all kinds of literature and learning. And Daniel could understand visions and dreams of all kinds. At the end of the time set by the king to bring them into his service, the chief official presented them to Nebuchadnezzar. The king talked with them, and he found none equal to Daniel, Hananiah, Mishael and Azariah; so they entered the king's service. In every matter of wisdom and understanding about which the king questioned them, he found them ten times better than all the magicians and enchanters in his whole kingdom. And Daniel remained there until the first year of King Cyrus.

— Daniel 1:3-9, 17-21

Sarah

Katie had several bloggers, vloggers, you-tubers—whatever you call them—that she enjoyed keeping up with on a regular basis. I often found her sitting in a chair with her eyes glued to the iPad. When I asked what she was watching, she named them as if she knew them personally and as if I knew who she was talking about. I asked, "Why do you spend so much time watching other people's lives?" She laughed and said, "They're funny," or "They're interesting," or "Their little girl is soooo cute!" I chuckled as I responded, "We're funny! Our family is interesting! And Daniel is super cute! What makes watching their life better than living ours? Maybe we should start a you-tube channel, Katie. Do you think people would want to watch our lives?" At that, she smirked and rolled her eyes.

We try to help our kids to navigate the world of social media as they become teenagers. We talk about the permanency of anything we post and the potential long-term ramifications. We talk about the ease at which we can make an unkind or inappropriate remark and the difficulty of interpreting messages without facial expressions or intonation. We talk a lot about selfies and the reason for posting them and what we hope people say about them.

I told Katie, "Your Instagram should be a lot more about you enjoying life and enjoying others than it is about your selfie and the comments that follow it." I don't want my kids to find their identity in what friends or acquaintances or even strangers say about them. I want them to find their confidence in Christ and in who God created them to be. Katie strived for this even though it was not always easy or the most natural inclination. She often wrote about "living life based on what Jesus thinks of me and not others," and "pleasing God over pleasing people." Her catchphrase—the tenet that formed the basis of her everyday—was FIND MY IDENTITY IN CHRIST.

◁

Katie

Every time I affirm my trust in God, I put a coin into God's treasury.

I build up equity in prep for days of trouble.

The more I trust him, the more he empowers me to do so.

PRACTICE trusting on QUIET days

So that when storms come, your trust balance will be sufficient to see you through.

STORE UP treasure in heaven.

PLACE YOUR TRUST IN HIM

Psalm 56:3-4

Matthew 6:20-21

When I am afraid, I put my trust in you. In God, whose word I praise— in God I trust and am not afraid. What can mere mortals do to me?

— Psalm 56:3-4

But store up for yourselves treasures in heaven, where moths and vermin do not destroy, and where thieves do not break in and steal. For where your treasure is, there your heart will be also.

— Matthew 6:20-21

Sarah

Katie's words about building equity each time she affirms her trust in God remind me of the words in the introduction that I shared many years ago with the young women I was discipling. Katie wrote, "that way when the storms come, your trust balance will be sufficient to see you through." Our trust equity is not built in the days of trouble. Our strength is not developed during the fight. In the midst of a violent storm is not the time to search for a place of security. Those steps happen before. We practice and prepare and learn to trust on quiet days.

Most days now, I wake up very early. Long before daylight. Long before breakfast. Long before the bedlam of a family busily preparing for the day. I crave the peace of that early morning. It is my time to pray, to read, to listen and to practice trusting God in the quiet. I pour some hot water and place a tea bag into a mug while I sit with God. I have several cups from which I enjoy drinking my morning tea, but my favorite is one from the Smiley Face Pottery company.

One winter during her tween years, Katie took a pottery course at a local pottery studio for a few weeks. She had the opportunity to work with clay, using her hands and the pottery wheel to mold a few pieces of pottery which she then painted and brought home. One piece was a thin vase made to look like a basket with a handle and painted a light brown. The other was a mug, painted a soft sea green, with a rough design on the outside and a rudimentary handle. On the bottom of both pieces is a clearly etched smiley face. A simple circle with closed eyes, a dot for a nose and a nice upwardly curved smile. Beneath the smile is a less visible carving that says, "KATIE." Although not inherently crafty, she really enjoyed the class, and she said that if she were to ever make her own pottery, she would call it *Smiley Face Pottery*. I told her that would be a perfect name!

I am so thankful for the smiley face on the bottom of my mug that reminds me to be still and to practice trusting God in the quiet of the day. And in the quiet days of life.

◁

Katie

We are all gifted.

Be who you is. If you ain't who you is, then you is who you ain't.

If your eye does what your foot does, then what is doing what your eye does?

In the same way, if you are trying to be another person, then you're not being yourself. Partner with Jesus. Partner with other followers. Point people to Jesus ♡

IDENTITY

Philippians 3:4-8

Paul was a person people looked up to. He had everything but he considered it trash compared to Jesus.

We have to find our identity in the Lord ♡

If someone else thinks they have reasons to put confidence in the flesh, I have more… But whatever were gains to me I now consider loss for the sake of Christ. What is more, I consider everything a loss because of the surpassing worth of knowing Christ Jesus my Lord, for whose sake I have lost all things. I consider them garbage, that I may gain Christ.

— Philippians 3:4-8

Sarah

C had and I believe very strongly in the power of influence in our children's lives. Not only do we aim to be intentional about how we influence our kids, but we are also keenly aware of the influence others wield. We know our kids are most likely to adopt and internalize the values of the people with whom they spend the most time, so we direct that time as much as possible. When they were small and learning so much about the world, we chose our babysitters with care. As they went to class at school and church, we showed up to read and check in. We have no desire to shelter our kids from people, but we absolutely want to know what character traits those people are modeling for our children. As they started into the age of extracurricular activities, our philosophy has always been that our kids will ultimately benefit more from time around the table with us than from any additional instruction or practice time. Although we recognize there is so much to learn from sports and music and creative activities, we know that they will also be influenced by those coaches and teachers and peers. Some of those instructors are fantastic but some are not, and we know character training and modeling is ultimately our responsibility.

As our kids get older, we also know our influence may change a little. Even though we think we are pretty cool, we recognize our kids probably will not carry that same sentiment into their teenage years. So, we begin early in their lives to widen the circle of influence. We intentionally expose, introduce and encourage them to connect with older friends and adults who will speak and model the same principles—just in a more with-it manner than we would. We want other people instilling the same values into our kids.

Therefore, on their 13th birthdays, we celebrate this. We acknowledge the teenage years as a season of looking more to others than to their parents, so we invite the people who comprise the circle of influence in their life to celebrate with us and to challenge and encourage our kids in a special way.

For Katie's 13th birthday, we invited her grandmothers and aunts, along with several of her friends, their mothers, and other women of various ages to an evening at our house. Each of these women already had a relationship with Katie that she respected, and we wanted to encourage those relationships to continue. After a dinner of lasagna and salad and homemade rolls, we all gathered around the room as Katie sat, slightly embarrassed, in a chair near the edge. Each woman brought a note she had written with words of affirmation and encouragement, along with charges and challenges to stay the course as the world began to shift around her. These women in Katie's circle of influence all encouraged her to be her own person—the woman she was gifted to be—but also to find her identity in Christ, not Instagram likes or another's approval. Then each woman closed with a reminder that they were for her. "I am here, Katie," they said, "for whatever you need." I knew they would be. She knew they would be. The women in that room, along with a few others, would be her strength, her compass, her circle of influence. They would point her to Jesus so that she could point others.

◁

Katie

> The Lord has done it this very day; let us rejoice today and be glad.
>
> — Psalm 118:24

> To this you were called, because Christ suffered for you, leaving you an example, that you should follow in his steps.
>
> — 1 Peter 2:21

View each day as an adventure planned out by God.

Don't perfectly plan out your day. God knows what will happen so just be attentive to Him.

Thank God for each day.

God is with me each moment, whether I know it or not.

A life lived close to God is always full of surprises.

Don't take the easiest path.

Follow WHEREVER God leads you.

The safest place to be is by His side!

Psalm 118:24

1 Peter 2:21

Sarah

Katie liked a little bit of adventure. She loved to go to the lake with her uncle Josh and his family and there she learned to rock climb and wake-surf behind a boat. She always looked forward to a week away at camp with new activities to try, and she adored serving in the nursery at church which certainly constitutes an adventure. I hoped to take her with me on a mission trip to Haiti around age 14. I knew she would love the opportunity to interact with the Haitian children and to serve in that way. However, I also knew feeding her in that setting would be challenging because, while Katie may have been adventurous in her life and her walk with God, she was much less adventurous in her eating habits. She was quite a picky eater.

Like a lot of kids, she loved carbs and did not eat many vegetables. As much as I tried, she mostly stuck with green beans for her primary veggie. Once, she decided she was going to learn to eat salad. "Because healthy people eat salad and I want to be healthy," she said. She started with one piece of lettuce on her plate and a plan to add a piece each day. I think she made it to six pieces of lettuce and three baby carrots, which she chewed for an incredibly long time while making bizarre faces, before she decided to give up on that venture.

She had an aversion to other foods most kids do enjoy, though. Like tacos. And spaghetti sauce. And homemade ooey-gooey macaroni and cheese (she preferred Velveeta). Perhaps the oddest food item Katie did not consume was chocolate. Chocolate! How does anyone not enjoy chocolate, right?!? And that is exactly what everyone said when she told them. Even knowing her, I always found it to be inconceivable. She did, however, like chocolate caramel truffle ice cream. How is that, you may ask. Well, she convinced her best friend to share it with her, so Katie ate the vanilla ice cream, even licking the caramel off, leaving the chocolate pieces for Thessa. What a friend!

Once, while grocery shopping with those two girls, Katie wondered aloud what we could possibly need as we headed down the candy aisle. I replied, "Chocolate. Because mothers who do not have chocolate eat children." Katie rolled her eyes, but I reassured her that I was confident her hormones would eventually drive her to appreciate the taste of fine chocolate.

◁

Katie

Knowledge of the Bible is good.

Luke 24:13-34

It's easy to get the wrong answer. Study the Bible!

The Gospel is the greatest love story ever told.

He died because He loves us!

Old Testament = New Testament concealed

New Testament = Old Testament revealed

If you want to grow, read the book of John.

Scripture isn't just a list of rules. It's a road map.

Fall in love with it! Dive in!

"About Jesus of Nazareth," they replied. "He was a prophet, powerful in word and deed before God and all the people. The chief priests and our rulers handed him over to be sentenced to death, and they crucified him; but we had hoped that he was the one who was going to redeem Israel. And what is more, it is the third day since all this took place.

When he was at the table with them, he took bread, gave thanks, broke it and began to give it to them. Then their eyes were opened, and they recognized him, and he disappeared from their sight. They asked each other, "Were not our hearts burning within us while he talked with us on the road and opened the Scriptures to us?"

— Luke 24:19-21, 30-32

For God so loved the world that he gave his one and only Son, that whoever believes in him shall not perish but have eternal life.

— John 3:16

Sarah

Katie loved to read. She was often reading several books simultaneously. Different genres, different lengths, different purposes. She read over FaceTime with her friend, Maddie, while Maddie lived in England. She read in the tree in the front yard where she could hide away among the leaves. She read while lying on her back on the trampoline in the sunshine. She read sitting across from her friend on her bed. She loved the hanging chair on our back deck that sits tucked into the corner, quiet and mostly unnoticed. She spent hours there in the warm weather, reading and eating popsicles. She tried several times to read in the hammock in the backyard, but she could never get past the insects that occasionally wanted to join her there.

Katie enjoyed mysteries and love stories, dramas and feel-good tales. She identified them as "daytime" books and "nighttime" books. Anything mysterious or frightening, anything that caused a little angst or fear, was dubbed a "daytime" book. Most other books could be "nighttime" books. She enjoyed her sleep and did not want any threat of anxiety interfering with it, but she also did not want to miss out on a great story. She said things like, "That's a great book! But it is *definitely* a daytime book."

Katie read lots of books, but she also read her Bible most days. Depending on the season of life and her schedule, she either woke up early in the morning or tucked herself into bed at night with her Bible and journal. I guess the Bible qualified as both a daytime book and a nighttime book. Sometimes she chose a book of the Bible (based on Chad's recommendation) and she used a specific study method to discover as much as possible from the passage. Sometimes she had a devotional or study she worked through. Katie craved truth and she learned to feed herself from God's Word. She did not simply accept what she was told; instead, she dove in, sought answers and fell in love with it.

◁

Katie

God's Word teaches us Courage and Boldness in Tough Times

Daniel 3:14-29

W Even if God doesn't save us, we still would never worship any other God. Nebuchadnezzar went from praising stone to praising God.

O They were more concerned about keeping commandment (no other gods), that they didn't care if it meant losing their life.

R Help me to stand up for what is right even if that means I have to give up something I love. It's a hard decision, but you'd make it with the snap of a finger. Please, help me to grow in my faith through your Word.

D In hard (dark) times, find God (light) & focus on what is RIGHT!

This journal entry follows a Bible study method called WORD.
W=Write the verse that stands out to you
O=Observe the key points
R=Relevant connections to your life
D=Declare what God teaches you

Shadrach, Meshach and Abednego replied to him, "King Nebuchadnezzar, we do not need to defend ourselves before you in this matter. If we are thrown into the blazing furnace, the God we serve is able to deliver us from it, and he will deliver us from Your Majesty's hand. But even if he does not, we want you to know, Your Majesty, that we will not serve your gods or worship the image of gold you have set up." Then Nebuchadnezzar was furious with Shadrach, Meshach and Abednego, and his attitude toward them changed. He ordered the furnace heated seven times hotter than usual and commanded some of the strongest soldiers in his army to tie up Shadrach, Meshach and Abednego and throw them into the blazing furnace.

So Shadrach, Meshach and Abednego came out of the fire, and the satraps, prefects, governors and royal advisers crowded around them. They saw that the fire had not harmed their bodies, nor was a hair of their heads singed; their robes were not scorched, and there was no smell of fire on them. Then Nebuchadnezzar said, "Praise be to the God of Shadrach, Meshach and Abednego, who has sent his angel and rescued his servants! They trusted in him and defied the king's command and were willing to give up their lives rather than serve or worship any god except their own God.

— Daniel 3:16-20, 26-28

Sarah

Every summer our church hosts a soccer camp in place of the traditional vacation Bible school. Big Kick Soccer Camp introduces a lot of kids in our communities to soccer and to Jesus. Katie had attended Big Kick Soccer since she was in preschool, but the summer before her seventh-grade year was the first time she was able to participate as a coach. That year, as a humble, sweet, little 12-year-old girl, she was paired up with Matt, a 30-something guy, to coach a team of four-year-olds. Matt had played the game for 30 years and had previously coached little kids' soccer, so he didn't have any worries. Katie, on the other hand, had never really coached, but she understood the game and was eager to help.

On the first day of camp, Katie and Matt met, collected the kids on their team and off they went. Before long, Big Kick was over for the night and, as far as Matt thought, they had accomplished their goal: the kids all had some fun and worked about as hard as any four-year-old was willing.

Day two. Just as smooth as day one. The kids were happy, no one got hurt and everyone was having a good time. Another successful day at Big Kick.

Day three. Considering the first two days, everything seemed normal to Matt. It was nice outside, and the kids were having fun chasing a soccer ball. Up to this point, Matt kind of drove the practices with Katie's help, and, in his opinion, the two of them had it all under control.

Then came snack time.

Katie and Matt were walking back with their kids and their snacks. She looked up at him and said, "You know we are supposed to be having God time after snack, right?" Apparently, he did not read the cliff notes, and she surely saw the look on his face, terrified that he had failed as a Big Kick coach. At that point in his life, Matt did not even want to discuss God aloud, not to mention effectively teach anyone—including a four-year-old. He had just barely gotten involved in church and was only beginning to learn about God himself.

Katie looked at him and said, "I'll take care of God time; you just coach soccer." He immediately made a deal with her. Twelve-year-old Katie proceeded to pull several preschoolers onto her tiny lap as she taught them—and Matt—about her Jesus. She was bold enough in her faith to take the reins from this man, and he was humble enough to let her. God used these moments in Katie's life to mature her. She may not have realized it then, but her courage was growing. Her love for God was becoming bolder. Her light was starting to shine brighter.

◁

Katie

Because you are my help, I sing in the shadow of your wings. I cling to you; your right hand upholds me.

— Psalm 63:7-8

Consider it pure joy, my brothers and sisters, whenever you face trials of many kinds, because you know that the testing of your faith produces perseverance. Let perseverance finish its work so that you may be mature and complete, not lacking anything.

— James 1:2-4

Let God help me through today.

The challenges I face are far too great for me to handle alone.

I'm keenly aware of my helplessness in the scheme of events I face.

I have the choice to doggedly go it alone or walk with God in humble steps of dependence.

This choice is continually before me.

trials are gifts from God

Remind me to rely on Him alone.

Psalm 63:7-8

James 1:2-4

"When your faith is tested, your endurance has a chance to grow!"

Sarah

I don't know the exact date that Katie wrote the words, "Let God help me through today. The challenges I face are far too great for me to handle alone." When she confronted the choice to "doggedly go at it alone or walk with God in humble steps of dependence," it was sometime before October 2016.

Early in October 2016, Katie had some vague complaints of feeling tired. She had developed a mild cough and complained of feeling slightly nauseated at breakfast one morning. Allergies, perhaps? She told me she woke up sweating a few nights, but I suggested that might be related to the three thick blankets on her bed. Of course, looking back, I question why I neglected those symptoms, but my kids are rarely ever sick, and I don't tend to jump on them with thermometers and worried expressions. We all feel worn out occasionally, viruses come and go, and she was in the middle of an especially busy season with school and sports. However, after she came home from volleyball practice saying that the coughing made it difficult to catch her breath, I became more concerned. That evening, she laid on the couch with a fever, snuggled up under her blanket. I began to suspect a mild pneumonia, likely acquired from a couple girls on her volleyball team who had recently been diagnosed with the same.

Katie was seen in her physician's office the next morning, but despite starting an antibiotic and inhaler, the mild cough and slight fevers continued, always worse in the evenings. Finally, after a few days of this, Dr. Liz assessed her again, changed her medications and sent her for an immediate chest X-ray. The radiology report came back right away as a complicated pneumonia with a pleural effusion, meaning that she had fluid accumulating around her right lung and limiting the air space available to breathe. Clinically, Katie looked okay, smiling through her cough and mild weakness. She certainly did not look as sick as the X-ray indicated. And how does a healthy 13-year-old girl suddenly develop such a complicated pneumonia anyway? After seeing her smile through her cough and with some prodding on my part, her physician reluctantly agreed to allow me to treat her at home, but I had to promise to return with her if she worsened at all.

Less than two full days later, Katie was at home catching up on make-up work from school when I walked into the house from a quick hair appointment. She began telling me about a movie she was watching, sharing lots of details. I noticed, however, that with every two or three words, she paused to take a breath. She did not act like she felt ill or fatigued, and she was almost giddy as she talked. When I asked her what she had been doing and why she was short of breath, she simply said she was excited about the movie. "Have you been exercising or doing anything else?" I asked. She said no and she denied feeling short of breath. It's amazing how kids can compensate and adjust to whatever their body throws at them. She looked so good and acted so fine that I stood there in my family room watching her. Was I overreacting? Was I assessing her correctly? Why did her appearance not align with the symptoms I had seen over the past week and with the chest X-ray?

I decided to run an errand and take her with me so I could keep an eye on her. As we were pulling out of the driveway, I watched her chest in the passenger seat and counted her respirations. Thirty-eight. At least twice as high as normal. She still insisted that she did not feel short of breath, but she was definitely worsening. She needed to be rechecked, and Dr. Liz instructed me to take her to the emergency room.

Oh, she was so mad when I told her where we were headed. "Why? I'm already on antibiotics!" she said. I hated to do it. I hoped I was overreacting. I told her to pack a change of clothes and a book "just in case we had to wait there a while." I was confident they would admit her for intravenous (IV) antibiotics, and I knew a chest tube was a real possibility if the fluid had not improved. In my mind, that was the worst-case scenario. This would not be fun, but we could do it.

Once in the emergency room, not only were her respirations fast, but her heart rate and temperature were significantly elevated. Her lab results were terrible, and the repeat chest X-ray looked worse as well. Everything indicated that her body was enlisting a lot of effort to fight something, but the identity of that something was still unknown. The physician immediately planned to admit her to the hospital for further treatment. The big decision seemed to be whether or not to place a chest tube. We sat in the emergency room for several hours as the surgical resident performed a bedside ultrasound, the phlebotomist took more blood, and the staff discussed her plan of care.

It seemed to be taking so long, and I was frustrated as to why they were having trouble making a decision. The nurses kept saying that the physicians were talking to the on-call surgeon and reviewing everything. First, they planned for CT scan that night and then chest tube placement. Then they said they would do the scan after they placed the chest tube. Then there was confusion as to where they would admit her: pediatric floor or pediatric intensive care unit (PICU). Finally, around

10:30pm, as we were settling into the PICU, the nurses informed me the decision had been made to wait until morning to place the chest tube in the operating room. "Okay," I said, "so she can eat now?" When they said no, I asserted, "Yes. If she is not going to the operating room until tomorrow, then she should be able to eat tonight." She was anxious and hungry after hours of waiting. This was the first of many chances I had to sincerely advocate for my kid, and the staff finally relented. So Katie ate a pepperoni roll we had brought from lunch and washed it down with—what seemed like—a pitcher of water.

Monitors, IVs and antibiotics. Operating room in the morning. Chest tube. CT scan. In my mind, the worst-case scenario had been admission and chest tube. It looked like that was certainly going to happen. I could do this. Although different when it's your own child, this was right in the range of normal work activity for me. And while perhaps not physically tough, Katie was definitely emotionally tough. She could do this, too.

I got very little sleep that night. I had difficulty getting comfortable in the recliner chair beside her bed, although it was probably as much mental discomfort as physical. Katie had her iPod by her head playing the radio station K-LOVE all night. I prayed and watched her, trying to sleep but not accomplishing much. The surgical resident came back in to check on her during the night. I asked him if they thought this large pleural effusion was due to the pneumonia, all of which seemed odd in an otherwise healthy 13-year-old girl. He simply said, "We presume, but we don't know." The thought of what else it could be really never crossed my mind at that point.

The next morning there was a lot of back and forth and what seemed like disorder about the plan for the day. Surgery then CT scan? Scan first and then surgery? What procedure were they performing again? Were we waiting on the attending surgeon or going straight to the operating room? At first, I was aggravated with all of the confusion. Then I began to realize that this was not confusion but, instead, lots of people trying to make sense of her presentation and move forward with the right decision. Finally, the resident explained the plan to take her for a CT scan first in order to rule out a mass. I let that blow right past me because I was convinced this scan was just to clarify what procedure would be most effective. I truly never considered there could actually be a mass in her chest.

Chad was on his way to the hospital, having just dropped off Daniel at preschool and picked up breakfast for me. As soon as the surgeon pulled up the CT images on a computer to discuss them, Chad walked through the doors of the PICU. I interrupted the surgeon to say, "Just a minute. Here comes my husband." So, as Chad stood there with a coffee in one hand and a Panera bag in the other, the surgeon informed us that Katie had a tumor in her chest. I always felt terrible that Chad was so completely caught off guard in that situation but, truly, so was I. We both just stood there, utterly confounded. He asked if we wanted to tell Katie or if we wanted him to explain to her the situation. I responded, "Um, I guess you can. I mean, I don't know what to say." So, very gently, the pediatric surgeon communicated to Katie about the tumor, the fluid, the biopsy and the chest tube. She was as stunned as Chad and I, and the three of us sat there for several quiet minutes, trying to process the words and the shock and the day ahead of us.

I had left my breakfast on the nurse's desk because I did not want Katie to see my food and certainly did not want to eat in front of her as she awaited surgery. After a few minutes, I excused myself to the waiting room with my bagel, but I could not eat. In a flood of tears, I made a few phone calls. One friend reassured me he would do whatever we needed, although he told me later he could not even understand the words I said. When I was able to recover my emotions a little, I returned to Katie's room. Within a few minutes, we were ushered into another room to meet the oncologist. She had lots of questions about Katie's health, family history and how these symptoms had transpired. As I cried, she handed me tissues. I liked her, but I did not like that she was on Katie's case. This was all becoming too real. Katie did not even have a diagnosis, but she already had an oncologist? I was having trouble fully comprehending the situation.

A few minutes later, Katie spoke for all of us when she simply asked, through tears, "What does this all mean?" As Chad and I sat on her bed, we told her the hard, but simple, truth: "We don't know. We know there is a mass of some kind in your chest but that's all we know. As soon as they can figure out what it is then we can decide what to do next. For now, let's just get this fluid off your chest so you can breathe better." After that, Katie did not appear to be overly anxious, and she diverted her attention to complaints of being hungry.

Throughout Katie's entire illness, we were always honest with her and with our other kids. We never avoided or covered the truth, but we were also very careful to give them only the information that they either needed or asked for. I answered every one of Katie's questions directly but simply. I never gave her more details than what she wanted to hear and process in that moment, but I never kept anything from her either.

In the anesthesia holding area, we were bombarded on all sides with people speaking and asking questions. One nurse anesthetist introduced herself as Megan, a "Winfield girl" (Winfield being our small hometown), and she began to ease Katie's anxiety a little. When Chad and I went to the waiting room, we found friends there waiting for us. As we rehashed the morning's events, I hung my head as if it was too heavy for my neck and rubbed my face in my hands, unable to fully grasp what was happening.

I left the hospital later that afternoon with a couple friends who had arrived just as we were getting Katie settled back into her room after surgery. My mental state must have been obviously impaired from the trauma of the day's events coupled with the lack of sleep because they insisted on driving me home. Chad stayed with Katie so I could be home with the other kids for the night. That evening, after dinner, I sat them on the couch as I told them what was happening with their sister. I explained that there were three things going on. First, she had pneumonia which was being treated with antibiotics. Second, she had fluid around her lungs which was being treated with a chest tube to drain it. Finally, I said, "She has something else in her chest and we don't know what it is, but when we find out what it is, we will do whatever we need to do to take care of it." They had only a few questions as that was mostly sufficient knowledge for them. As I reiterated these three things to my kids, I added: "If someone tells you anything different than this, remember, they don't know. *I know.* I know what's going on with Katie, not anyone else." I did not want them hearing adults or other kids at school asking or saying words like *cancer* or *tumor* and increasing their worry when we really did not know anything at this point.

My oldest son, Aaron, was then 15 years old, so I offered a little more information to him than I did to the younger three. He could process more and deserved the chance to do so. I took him off to the side of the kitchen and explained that the "thing" in her chest was a tumor of some sort. "Does that mean cancer?" he asked with concern. I replied, "Well, we don't know for certain, but probably." He took a big breath and headed out the back door for a long walk by himself.

Once I laid myself down in bed that night, I fell asleep quickly and slept soundly, utterly exhausted. When I awoke in the morning, my first thought was, "I slept so good." Then I immediately remembered Katie and my heart just sank. It felt so heavy. I literally clutched my chest because it felt like my heart was breaking. I rolled my body out of bed and sat on the couch for some time. I struggled to pray, simply saying, "Jesus," over and over again. My prayers became mostly cries of anguish at that point. I started saying things to God like, "You can't take her from me!" and "I love her, too!" and "If you need to teach me something, don't use her to do it!" Eventually, I tried to walk up the steps to the kids' bedrooms to awaken them for the day, but the words spilled out again, "You can't take her from me!" In tears, I fell to my knees there on the steps, as God spoke to me in the most audible voice I have ever heard from him. He said, "Shhhhh. This isn't about you." So I cried out louder, "But I don't want to lose her!" And very gently, he said again, "Shhhhh. This isn't about you. This is her story. This is Katie's story."

In tears, I stood up. And that's the last time I said those words to him. Because he was right. This is her story. And she is *his* daughter.

◁

Katie

Be still in the light of God's presence.

There is no force in the universe as powerful as His love.

I am constantly aware of limitations: mine and others'.

There is NO limit to God's love.

It fills all space, time and eternity.

Someday I will see God face to face!

Then I'll be able to experience fully how wide and long and high and deep is His love for me.

If I were to experience that now, I'd be overwhelmed to the point of feeling crushed.

For now the knowledge of His loving presence is sufficient enough to carry me through each day.

1 Corinthians 13:12

Ephesians 3:16-19

For now we see only a reflection as in a mirror; then we shall see face to face. Now I know in part; then I shall know fully, even as I am fully known.
— 1 Corinthians 13:12

I pray that out of his glorious riches he may strengthen you with power through his Spirit in your inner being, so that Christ may dwell in your hearts through faith. And I pray that you, being rooted and established in love, may have power, together with all the Lord's holy people, to grasp how wide and long and high and deep is the love of Christ, and to know this love that surpasses knowledge—that you may be filled to the measure of all the fullness of God.
— Ephesians 3:16-19

me at 3

turn your face to the sun and the shadows
will fall behind you

big sis & little sis 💜

any day spent with you is my favorite day, so
today is my new favorite day

momma giggles :)))))

just keep running, running, running

spelling bee with a great friend

from then until now, you guys are so amazing
and never cease to make me smile, ily ♥

the greatest summers are full of pool trips, popsicles and best friends

love these girlies ♥

best small group leader ever :)

BIG KICK!!!!!!

action shot :))))

i have the best friends. thank you for celebrating with me :)

love celebrating my 13th birthday with these ladies ♥

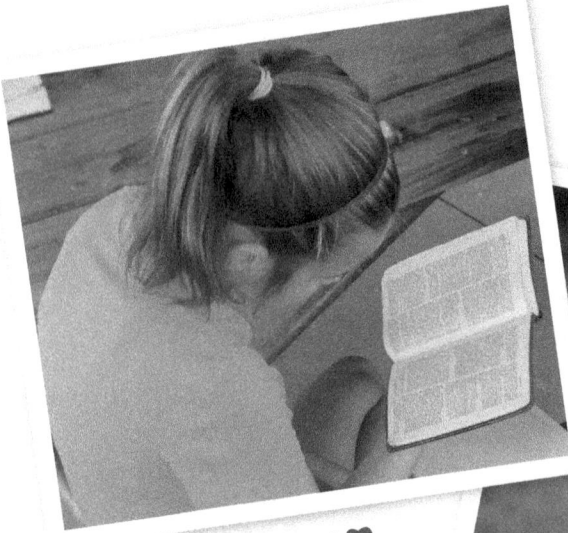
spending time with God ♥

say cheese :))))

can't imagine a life without you guys ♥

PART 2

A Diagnosis

Katie

What on earth am I here for?

Sarah

*W*hat is this? Is this cancer? What kind of cancer? Is it treatable? So, when do we start the treatment? Why is it taking so long? Why can't we do something now? As we waited on these answers from the doctors, I also had questions for God: What is this? What are you doing, God? What is the point of this? Do all things really happen for a reason? And why Katie? Is there really purpose in this? What on earth are we here for?

Lots and lots of questions. And no good answers. In fact, there were very few answers at all. We seemed to move sloth-like through a scene we wished would pass quickly. We yearned for answers, a diagnosis, a treatment plan. We wanted to *do* something. To help the situation, to manage the parts of it, to control the outcome. Just do something… anything. Yet we are not called human doings. We are called human *beings*. And ironically, just *being* is one of the hardest tasks of our humanness.

While we waited for a confirmed diagnosis for Katie, we did a lot of being. Just being present. Friends had dropped off things to occupy our time: movies to watch, puzzle books to complete, books to read. Nonetheless, we were also beginning to learn how to simply be present with each other and with God. This proved to be an important lesson for the coming year as well as for all of life. Sometimes, the waiting… the time in between… the opportunity to just be… is a gift.

Later in her illness, we coined a phrase that became our mantra: *We do not know what tomorrow will bring, but today can still be a good day.* This daily refrain seemed to give purpose to the present while pushing away the fear of the unknown. The fear that made my legs quiver when I tried to stand. The fear that left me nauseated in the bathroom. The fear that threatened to destroy my life, my family, my hope, my faith.

I prayed fervently when I could. I earnestly asked God to make this be nothing. One big mass of nothing. I believed he could do that. "Show off, God!" I prayed. "Show yourself." But the fear. The fear that filled that space of waiting incapacitated me at times. I began to rely heavily on the prayers of others because my own words had vanished. I told a group of friends, "You have to believe for me because I am overcome by doubt." I received replies such as this one: "Fear not. You and your family are surrounded by prayer warriors in full combat gear doing battle to protect you. Occasionally, a demon of fear will get through but remember, we are here." It was not long after receiving those words of encouragement that my fears began to subside. The prayers were almost tangible. It was as if I felt their arms on my back holding me up to stand.

Katie's diagnosis came on October 25, 2016. Through various comments made by the nurses and physicians, I had already determined they were concerned this was a very aggressive cancer. So, when the pathology results showed Hodgkin Lymphoma, I was almost relieved. In fact, a physician friend stopped by the hospital just as we received this news and, as I hugged her, I said, "This is okay, right? I mean, if it had to be cancer, this was the best option. We can treat this. Right?" And she, too, seemed relieved.

Hodgkin Lymphoma is one of the most treatable blood cancers with a short treatment regimen and a high success rate. This was manageable. Six months of chemotherapy. Possible radiation at the end. A really hard year, but then it would be part of her past. That's what I told Katie. That's how I spun it. That's how we were gonna play the game of cancer.

And she received it. She tucked that diagnosis under her arm like a football, put her head down and ran with it. And we started to cheer. It would be a tough route with obstacles to navigate, but, in the end, we believed she would win.

◁

Katie

Continue on the path with God enjoying His presence even in adversity.

God is always BEFORE me & ALONGSIDE me.

The one who goes ahead of me, opening the way, is the same one who stays close & never lets go of our hand.

God is not subject to limitations of time or space.

He is everywhere at every time,

always working on my behalf.

TRUST GOD & LIVE CLOSE TO HIM!

Sarah

"Be strong and courageous. Do not be afraid or terrified because of them, for the Lord your God goes with you; he will never leave you nor forsake you." Deuteronomy 31:6

Katie chose this verse for the T-shirts created in her support. She taught herself to believe that God's presence is with us even in adversity. And that he goes BEFORE and ALONGSIDE us. We needed this reminder as we continued forward.

We were relieved to get the chemotherapy treatments started so as to prevent any further growth of the tumor or accumulation of fluid around her lungs. However, saying the word *chemotherapy* also makes the diagnosis a little more real. I sat beside her in the hospital room and watched as the nurses prepared to start her regimen for the day. The chemotherapy medicine is sent from a special pharmacy department where it is mixed and checked and rechecked and triple checked. Then, after the nurse puts on special gloves and a special gown and maybe even a mask, she brings it into the room in a special bag. She uses special IV tubing to infuse it into Katie's port (a port is a vascular access point for chemotherapy). It's all so *special*. I watched as all of these precautions were taken with the chemotherapy medicine now entering my child's body. No one else wanted to touch it, but my Katie was getting the full force of it. This vicious medication with the cutesy nickname, chemo, was infusing directly into her bloodstream. And we were eager for it to do so because chemo kills cancer cells. Cancer cells. Cancer. Oh, crud, for a few minutes I had forgotten. My child has cancer.

◁

Katie

Mark 10:17-22

Philippians 3:7-8

Jesus tells the man to get rid of everything.

You may not have to do that in life but nothing should be of more importance than God.

Are you ok with losing EVERYTHING?

Don't take what you have for granted. Consider the story of Job.

Love God with all your ♡ heart, soul, mind.

God will NEVER fail you!

Love others as yourself.

Be thankful.

Jesus looked at him and loved him. "One thing you lack," he said. "Go, sell everything you have and give to the poor, and you will have treasure in heaven. Then come, follow me." At this the man's face fell. He went away sad, because he had great wealth.

— Mark 10:21-22

But whatever were gains to me I now consider loss for the sake of Christ. What is more, I consider everything a loss because of the surpassing worth of knowing Christ Jesus my Lord, for whose sake I have lost all things. I consider them garbage, that I may gain Christ...

— Philippians 3:7-8

Sarah

For Katie, losing her hair was the epitome of losing EVERYTHING. To be right in the middle of discovering your identity, building stronger relationships with peers, learning to express your personality and define where your beauty lies—and then to lose a part of you that is significant to all of that. Whew. That's a big hit.

Hair loss for a teenage girl might be one of the most detrimental components of cancer treatment. The chemotherapy medications used in treatment attack the cancer cells, but they attack other fast-multiplying cells in the body as well—for instance, cells in the gastrointestinal tract, the blood, and hair follicles. This explains why many chemotherapy medications cause nausea, anemia, decreased immunity, and, yes, hair loss.

While none of the side effects are pleasant and while each one impacts people differently, the hair loss alone can be disruptive on so many levels. First, it generally identifies you as a cancer patient. Like many people, Katie hated that. She did not want anyone (friends, relatives, or even strangers) to treat her differently because she had cancer. She did not even want to treat herself differently because of her cancer. She refused to allow a diagnosis to define her identity. Second, it changes your entire appearance. Hair gives a sense of uniqueness to one's appearance and, we hope, adds some component to physical attractiveness. It even provides an opportunity to express a bit of your personality.

When Katie was first diagnosed and we knew the hair loss would follow, I had the idea to have a hair cutting party. Here was my plan: Katie would cut her long, straight, light brown hair with the red Kool-Aid tips into a short bob, and we would invite friends or family that wanted to cut their hair in support to join us. Our hairdresser friend, Jacquelyn, would bring her scissors to the house for the afternoon and offer her services. Katie did not actually give her consent, but I pushed it through. She said to me, "I don't know why you keep calling it a party. This is not a party." That was before I knew how to acknowledge the pain; back then I was still trying to "look at the positive."

Well, it turned out that Katie was right. It was not a party after all. It was awful. Just flat awful. Some of her friends came. A few got their hair trimmed, and a couple cut theirs into short new styles. For most of the afternoon, no one knew what to say and it was way too quiet as everyone just sat around looking at each other. When Katie finally got on the stool to have her hair cut, everyone just watched. She hated it. I didn't know what to do. No one knew what to say. And, at some point in the midst of all this "fun," she also passed out. It was definitely not a party. In fact, it might have been the worst idea I ever had. Despite my attempts to help, it was not the least bit helpful to Katie.

With the impending hair loss upon her, Katie became determined to get a wig. We talked about the pros and cons of it, and she was convinced that she wanted to mask the outward and unmistakable signs of her cancer treatment with a wig. She craved normalcy in the midst of all of this. Someone gave us money explicitly for the purpose of buying a wig, so we went shopping for one that suited her. She picked out a couple to try on. But they didn't look like her hair. They didn't feel like her hair. It only took a few minutes to figure out that a wig was not going to work. The tears came pretty quickly for both of us. We bought a few hats on our way out the door to show our appreciation for the shop owner's help, but it was another really terrible day. This journey would not be easy, and it was just the beginning.

With chemo treatment, as the hair follicles let loose and the hair begins to fall out, it causes the head to hurt. The scalp just aches all over. As if anyone with cancer needs something else to hurt. Interestingly enough, once all the hair falls out—or if it is shaved off—the ache subsides. Katie wanted nothing of the head shaving experience, though, so she endured the painful days of finding handfuls of hair in her hat as she removed it each morning. When her hats went through the wash, I stood in the laundry room, picking out the remaining little hairs from the fibers. It was a feeble and helpless act that made almost no difference, but what else could I do? I could no longer offer to brush or braid or curl my girl's hair, so I lovingly and quietly removed each fine hair that might irritate or itch her now soft scalp.

Long before all the hair was gone, Katie started wearing hats. I cut my long hair down to a couple inches and chose the same plan. Around this time, we had a wedding to attend. She asked what I was going to wear with the long, navy blue dress I had picked out, and I pointed to a cute little cotton hat in a matching hue. "I'm just going to wear a hat with some earrings," I said, nonchalantly. With that, she did not hesitate a bit to put on a sweet little dress and a hat to match. She told her friend, "I'll just tell people that my mom is the one who is sick." Fine with me. Her first big outing as a cancer patient. She could do this, I thought.

No one was permitted to see Katie's bald head—not strangers, not family, not friends—and Katie did not see it either. In fact, I am almost certain she never looked at it. Initially, I encouraged her to face her appearance, thinking it would be impossible for her to avoid seeing it for months. But I already told you this girl had fierce determination. She did not want others to see her as ill because she did not see herself that way. Physically or psychologically. Instead of showers, she took baths. She wore her hat into the tub, removed it only briefly to wash her head with a washcloth, and then replaced the hat before she stepped out. She avoided her appearance in the mirror while changing her hats. She even slept in them. When her hair was nearly gone, she told me she could tell there was only a tuft left on the top of her head. I offered to trim it with scissors so it would no longer bother her. She agreed, but she found a spot in the center of my room where no mirrors could see her, and she told me very sternly, "Do it quickly and don't make any faces when you take off my hat." Hats became a part of her personality after that. A way to accessorize while deterring attention. She had many she hand-picked but so many more were given to her. Playful hats, comfy hats, hats with logos and hats to match every outfit. Most were beanies in various forms. She always surprised me when she wore the ones with the pom-pom on top, but those were her favorites. The maroon one with the brown pom-pom. The soft pink one. The white one. The floppy snow man hat that showed a fun side of her personality. The red and white hat she wore to all the Christmas parties. And the variegated one that matched everything. It took a while, but eventually she added baseball caps to her hat repertoire. She wore a headband around the bottom rim of the cap in the back so that no part of her bald head could be seen. It was super important to Katie that her head be covered. She had no desire for pity or to be identified by her cancer.

For the rest of her life, Katie was never without a hat. It makes me really sad to write that. She asked me once, about four months into her first round of treatment, how long I thought her hair would be by the time she started high school in the fall. I estimated maybe one to two inches. I know she was hoping for much more as she looked at me with tears pooling in her eyes and quietly asked, "Is that all?" She just bowed her head and let the tears run down her cheeks. She struggled to accept my less than optimistic answer that day, but little did we know that she would go on to lose her hair again. And again.

◁

Katie

Matthew 5:13

When you run a lot, you lose natural salt. Without salt, your body cannot stay hydrated. Without a relationship with Jesus, you can't absorb and learn from his Word.

Let others see God through you.

I need to truly give my life to God, and I'm a little afraid.

God is impacting my sport through me.

I BLEED GOD!!

You are the salt of the earth. But suppose the salt loses its saltiness. How can it be made salty again? It is no longer good for anything. It will be thrown out. People will walk all over it

— Matthew 5:13 (NIrV)

Sarah

Katie got her first Fitbit when she was twelve years old. It was the simplest version, but she loved being able to challenge herself and almost anyone else. She set up competitions between herself and her grandma, aunts, cousins, and friends. Most of the people she competed against were closer to my age than hers, but she really enjoyed this little relationship she built with them through Fitbit. Her uncle Joey beat her one time in his number of steps. He never beat her again, but he also never let her forget that one day. She walked up and down our stairs at the end of the evening or marched in place while she helped in the kitchen if she needed "just a few more steps." There was only one person she would not challenge—a family friend named Nicolina – who logged an astounding number of steps per day.

Katie was so excited to get a newer model Fitbit for Christmas the year she was undergoing chemo. She bought bands in every color to wear with it. She also convinced the other kids to pool their money at Christmas to buy a Fitbit for both Chad and me. Unfortunately, we hardly wore them, and she and Aaron always gave us grief about how much money they spent for a gift we didn't appreciate. I tried to participate but I was really only doing it for her, and after Katie worsened, all the fun of counting steps was gone for me.

As I read her journal and see her words, "God is impacting my sport through me," I think, *not only your sport, Katie, but God is impacting people through you.* She even used her Fitbit to create relationships and then leveraged those relationships for God. She wanted to sweat and bleed God, and it was almost impossible to look at Katie and not see HIM.

◁

Katie

I am God's for all time and into eternity.

No power can deny my inheritance in heaven.

I'M SO SECURE!

Even if I falter as I journey through life, God will never let go of my hand!

My future is absolutely secure.

Don't approach the day as a blank page to fill up.

Be on the lookout for all that God is doing.

This sounds easy, but it requires a deep level of trust.

GOD'S WAY IS PERFECT!

Psalm 37:23-24

Psalm 18:30

The Lord makes firm the steps of the one who delights in him; though he may stumble, he will not fall, for the Lord upholds him with his hand.

— Psalm 37:23-24

As for God, his way is perfect: The Lord's word is flawless; he shields all who take refuge in him.

— Psalm 18:30

Sarah

God's original creation of humanity was intended to reflect and represent his own relationship with Jesus and his relationship with us. While we can learn of God's love for us through other ways, witnessing his love through our own father is one of the best ways to begin to understand it. Though not perfect by any means, Chad has been a model of God's love in the way he fathers our kids. He enjoys them, challenges them and walks beside them. He did this for Katie, giving her a sense of security in her relationship with him. The trust she had in her earthly father fostered her trust in her Heavenly Father.

Katie and Chad are similar in so many ways. Quiet yet extroverted. Dedicated to excellence. And both are fascinated with math, Jesus and a good book. One day early in her illness, as Chad was leaving the house for work and Katie was sitting on the end of the couch, he offered her a fist bump and said, "Wonder Twin Powers… Activate!" She gave him a sideways look and a smirk as she put out her fist. At first, it was just something silly to say, a random memory from his childhood of Saturday mornings watching *Super Friends*, but it soon became a sweet phrase of connection between them. And it kind of made sense. They were sort of twin-ish in the ways they related to life and, in many ways, they did make each other better. He often spoke their tagline when he walked out of her hospital room or when he returned, as if he could impart some of his own physical strength into her frail body. *Wonder twin powers… activate*. Perhaps it was more than physical strength that he ultimately shared with her.

Whenever Katie was asked to write about who she admired or someone she looked up to, she always referenced her dad. She cited his patience, his kindness and his ability to balance many roles in life. She asked for his insight on Bible verses she read and for his opinion on posts she wrote for her blog. Sure, they had similar physical features, but she had no idea how much she looked like him on the inside.

One of the most obvious similarities between Katie and Chad was their sense of humor. They laughed at the same corny jokes and puns and often started into a belly laugh that was unrelenting. As the rest of us stood around with puzzled looks about what was so funny, the two of them sat on the couch, barely able to catch their breath, as they threw their heads back in hilarity. Their giggles would begin to calm until one looked at the other, sending them into fits all over again. Even when I didn't understand the cause of the laughter, I enjoyed watching the two of them snicker and snort and leak tears of happiness.

One evening when Katie was in the hospital awaiting her initial diagnosis, I was preparing to go home with the other kids while Chad stayed there with her. As I was leaving the room, something got them started giggling. Katie began to cackle as she said, "Oh Daddy, not too much, my chest tube hurts!" I smiled as I quipped to Chad, "Don't make her laugh too hard! She needs to breathe!" Because breathing is required for living.

Sometimes, though, so is laughter.

◁

Katie

PRAYER JOURNAL

T.   M.A.W. & S.J.G foundations

T.   meal providers

O.   Travis & leukemia

O.   you-tubers

M.   counts come up ↑

M.   no relapse

Make-A-Wish and Sweet Julia Grace are foundations who provided something special for Katie during her illness.

Sarah

A couple years ago, I was a little frustrated with my kids tending toward prayers of big, generic nothingness rather than true conversations with God about real people and events and frustrations in their lives. They often prayed (and still do sometimes): "God, thank you for a good day and good food and help us to have a good night's sleep and a good day tomorrow." Okay, yea, like what does that even mean? Big ol' good American nothingness. I mean, I know they are just kids and I can give them credit for being willing to pray out loud and direct their thoughts toward God, but I want their relationship with their Heavenly Father to be more than that. More honest, more loving, more intentional. More about a dialogue and less about "gimme a bunch of generic good stuff."

So, I devised a method to help them focus a bit more. I called it a TOM prayer, and then stretched it into a TOM² prayer. Simple and easy. But the most important component is to be specific.

T is for thanks. Express gratitude for two (remember, we squared it) specific people or situations in your life. None of this: *Thank you for my friends* or *Thank you for a good day.* More like this: *God, thank you for Mrs. Dillow who is always happy to listen to me before class starts* or *Thanks for helping Sophie's puppies to get adopted by good families.* This is intentional thanksgiving.

O is for others. Pray for two specific people in specific ways. *Help David (the Compassion child we sponsor) and his family in Kenya to have enough money. Take care of Travis and heal his cancer. Please keep Uncle Dean safe as he goes on a long climbing trip.* This is intentional intercession for others.

M is for me. Think about what is going on in your life, what you are feeling, what you are worried about, what you are excited for, and bring God into that. *I am having trouble falling asleep because I am afraid, so please help me to know you are with me and I don't have to be afraid. I want to do well in my piano lesson tomorrow, but I forgot to practice, so help me to do okay and then to remember to practice hard next week.* This is intentional reflection.

Katie has many journal entries listing TOM and tagging various names and requests. It makes me smile to read them and catch a glimpse into her dialogue with God. To read of her giving thanks for good results on her blood work and opportunities to visit with friends. To feel just a bit of her struggle as she prayed against her own relapse or reflected on returning to school. To know that she prayed for the you-tubers she watched, her friends, families from church, her doctors. She seemed to be able to give her fears to God while choosing to see the blessings of others. During Katie's toughest year, she prayed for the people who were a part of her life. What a blessing. What a challenge. I wonder how God used her prayers in our lives.

Katie

Matthew 14:22-33

Peter walks on water.

God wants you to take steps of faith, even if it's scary.

Peter stepped out of the boat because he had faith that it was God.

As long as we keep our focus on Jesus, we'll accomplish much.

Shortly before dawn Jesus went out to them, walking on the lake. When the disciples saw him walking on the lake, they were terrified. "It's a ghost," they said, and cried out in fear. But Jesus immediately said to them: "Take courage! It is I. Don't be afraid."

"Lord, if it's you," Peter replied, "tell me to come to you on the water."

"Come," he said. Then Peter got down out of the boat, walked on the water and came toward Jesus. But when he saw the wind, he was afraid and, beginning to sink, cried out, "Lord, save me!" Immediately Jesus reached out his hand and caught him. "You of little faith," he said, "why did you doubt?" And when they climbed into the boat, the wind died down. Then those who were in the boat worshiped him, saying, "Truly you are the Son of God."

— Matthew 14:25-33

Sarah

Katie and I sat in the Children's Cancer Center at our local hospital. I just think a place like that should not even exist, but there we were. Her white blood cells were pretty low but still deemed high enough for chemo to proceed. The first medication finished. Doxorubicin is red and looked like Kool-Aid as it made its way through the IV tubing and into her body. We laughed about it because we had to. Along with all the other medications in her regimen, it made her hair fall out and wreaked havoc on her blood cells, but it kills cancer. So, we had a deep love/hate relationship with it.

This was the last anticipated round of chemo. We had a lot of gratitude for that. Final scans were scheduled. The port would be removed from her chest after that. We did not know exactly when or where the tunnel ended, but we thought we saw light ahead of us. *Please, God, let that be daylight ahead of us. We are ready for the night to be over.*

Some days I wrote and journaled in a solitary effort to encourage myself and to remind myself of what I believed.

I wrote these words:

Faith is more than just believing that God is able or capable of doing something.

Faith calls us to believe in the character of God, including his goodness and generosity.

Katie wrote these words:

God wants you to take steps of faith, even if it's scary.

Peter stepped out of the boat because he had faith that it was God.

As we stepped out of the boat each day, walking forward into the unknown, we both relied heavily on our faith that God could do what he said he could do. But we also knew he might not. He could but he might not. And that is the point at which faith becomes something more. More than believing in God's capabilities, mature faith believes in his character. God is good, faithful and full of love. Even when he doesn't do what we believe he can do.

◁

Katie

Learn to live above circumstances.

That requires focused time with God.

Trouble and distress are a part of this world.

Only God's life in me can empower me to face these problems with good cheer.

As I sit quietly in God's presence, He shines peace into my troubled mind and heart.

Little by little, I am freed from earthly shackles and lifted up above my circumstances.

Rest in God's Presence receiving JOY no one can take away from you.

John 16:22

John 16:33

So with you: Now is your time of grief, but I will see you again and you will rejoice, and no one will take away your joy.

— John 16:22

"I have told you these things, so that in me you may have peace. In this world you will have trouble. But take heart! I have overcome the world."

— John 16:33

Sarah

As American Christians, we sometimes think God should protect us from everything that hurts in this world. However, as long as we live in a place wrought by the brokenness of sin, we will have brokenness in our lives. Pain, frustration, distress, struggle. Jesus said in John 16:33: "In this world you will have trouble." For now, trouble is part of earth. But he also said, "Take heart! I have overcome the world." Taking heart means that we can live above the trouble and the pain. Not in ignorance of it. Not in reluctant acceptance. Not in concession to the brokenness. But in peace… in good cheer… in JOY. It will not happen naturally because we cannot do it on our own. We have not overcome the trouble in this world—but Jesus has. So, living above my circumstances requires that he be in me which requires that I rest in him.

Katie returned to school as soon as the scan results came back negative and the oncologist cleared her. Throughout Katie's illness, I tried to allow her to live above her circumstances as much as possible. After that horrid hair-cutting party, I decided I could not control what cancer took from her, but I could control what I took from her. When she wanted to go ice-skating with her friends, I said yes (as long as her blood counts were reasonable). When she asked to go to the basketball game and sit in a crowd of people, I said yes (as long as she stayed away from anyone coughing or sniffling). And when she wanted to walk the half mile home from school every day, I said yes (as long as she felt strong enough). She refused to allow cancer to restrict her from what she would normally do and, as much as I wanted to protect her, I agreed with her desire to stand up against this ugly opponent.

But then she began to complain of back pain. We talked to her pediatrician, a physical therapist and her oncologist. All evidence pointed to a muscle strain due to carrying that backpack full of books each day. I was concerned, but I convinced myself this was just anxiety trying to rule my life. As I laid ice packs and heated washcloths on her back, I reminded myself that both the CT scan and the PET scan had been clear just a few weeks ago. *Go away, fear. Go away.*

Katie went to a TobyMac concert with her friend Micayla on Saturday night, but she ended up sitting in her chair throughout most of the concert because of the back pain. I knew she was tired the following morning, but something just seemed wrong to me. Later that afternoon, I watched her as she sat at a lunch gathering.

No smiling. No interacting. And then… then I noticed her breathing. *Damn. No. It's not fast. I won't even count the respirations because it can't be. It isn't. Not again. Nope.*

We soon left the picnic and headed home. She said she was tired and crawled into my bed to take a nap, pulling the covers up to her chest. My hand brushed her skin. It was hot. Flushed from being outside? Already warming up under the blanket? It couldn't be a fever. No way is this a cancer-related fever. *I won't even check it. Because it's not a fever. Right? I mean, it's not. She just had a clear scan. The steri-strips are still on her chest from the port removal last week. Last week! See? It isn't. I won't live in fear. I won't.*

I left the house for a quick errand. I had to walk away from the situation. I was only gone 10 minutes when Chad called. "Katie has a fever," he said. My head dropped. Something was definitely wrong.

Katie and I walked into the oncology clinic the next morning together, feeling completely defeated. She kept saying, "I know it's back. I know it is." Great big tears were rolling down her cheeks. I could not argue much. I tried to consider the other possibilities, but I knew it, too. The oncologist attempted to smile and reassure us, but she knew it, too. After labs and X-rays, we went home while the physician's office argued with our insurance company in an attempt to get another scan approved as soon as possible. Of course, the insurance balked because none of it made sense. Why should they pay for another scan when the one just a few weeks ago declared her cancer free?

By Tuesday morning, Katie was becoming increasingly short of breath. I was scheduled to go to work later that morning—I had just returned to work when she returned to school—so I dropped her off at Chad's office at the church. I told her to just lay on the couch and take it easy. Before I left, I walked into the staff meeting and informed Chad that she was not well and would need to go to the hospital if she worsened whatsoever. My entire body felt so heavy. I could barely lift my head. There was this pit inside me. My eyes filled with tears as the staff prayed for her and for us. I could not even make eye contact with anyone as I stood to leave. The awareness of it all was incomprehensible.

Just as we feared, within a few hours Chad took her to the emergency room at the local pediatric hospital. I left my shift as soon as I could, never to return. The following morning, Katie was taken to the operating room where the surgeon opened up the exact same incision he had used less than two weeks prior, placing a new port in the same place as the one he had just removed. Another biopsy. Another chest tube.

As Chad and I sat in the waiting room, leaning into one another, it was so surreal. Eerily familiar. Same symptoms. Same surgeon. Same procedures. Same diagnosis. *What is happening?* I wondered over and over again.

The next few days were the beginning of a long nightmare. We were back to managing her chest tube which drained fabulous for the first day and then almost not at all after that. Her respiratory rate hovered at three times normal for most hours of the day. Despite my questions and urgings, everyone blamed her fever… her anxiety… her pain. I asked why the chest tube wasn't draining… why can't we just pull the fluid off with a syringe… why is there no improvement in the X-rays? What are we going to do next? No answers. Finger pointing. This one will talk to the surgeon. That one will talk to the family practice residents. This one will talk to the oncologist. I laid beside her all day and night to help her pace her breathing. "Just breathe, Katie. Just breathe. Big slow breaths," I said. I monitored her oxygen. I helped her to the bedside commode. I reported her abnormal assessments. The nurses seemed to defer to me because I was both mom and nurse. Not fair. Not fair. "Somebody listen to me! She can't compensate like this forever! Her body will tire out. We have treated her fever and her pain and her anxiety and she is still struggling!!"

Upon my request, the oncology resident came to her room and attempted to address my concerns. As he tried to convince me she could be transported for an imaging study, still maintaining that her rapid respirations were related to her anxiety, I stood with my arms folded across my chest and just shook my head at him. Her body was exhausted from working so hard for so long, and I did not understand how no one could see that besides me. At that very moment Katie started to crash. As the resident stepped aside, I smacked the call light button on the wall and shouted into the intercom, "I need a non-rebreather mask now and call PICU!" That day we had a nurse who could see beyond what the residents were overlooking, and she stood with me in demanding that something more be done. Katie was then moved to the pediatric intensive care unit (PICU) which helped the situation a little bit through hi-flow oxygen, closer monitoring, and a strong bedside nurse to advocate for us.

Up to that time, I had tried to let the medical and nursing staff care for my daughter. I did not desire to be ugly or aggressive or to micro-manage her care, but I was done with that. Done. And I was mad. It was then that my friend Carly squarely said to me, "You can be sad later but today, today, you stand up and you advocate for your daughter." Despite my exhaustion, I rallied the fight inside me, and I let my anger override my sadness as I took a more direct role in her care. At one point, after a diagnostic test I had requested several days prior was finally ordered, I placed my finger in the physician's face and said, "I asked for that test to be done days ago. And if it comes back positive now, so help me, I will have someone's head on a platter."

The first night in PICU at our local pediatric hospital, the medical staff told us there was nothing else they could do for Katie. They simply did not have the research or specialty support for her situation. At that point, we made the decision to move her to Cincinnati Children's Hospital. It took about 36 hours to get everything accepted and ready for transfer, including intubating her in order to manage her respiratory status during the flight. Katie had been only minimally interactive for the prior few days because it literally took every ounce of energy she had to breathe. The space in her lungs was almost completely filled up with infection and the space around her lungs was filling with fluid, so her lung capacity was very, very small. When the small diameter chest tube was finally replaced with a large one to accommodate the drainage of fluid, Katie immediately lost nearly two liters of pleural fluid. Two liters is a lot to come off that little chest.

By the time Katie arrived in Cincinnati via helicopter, her body was in shock. Immediately there was a PICU attending physician, two physician fellows, a medical resident, and several registered nurses working around her bed for a couple hours. If I had any questions before as to whether or not she needed this level of care, I had no doubt now. She was so very sick. She was receiving aggressive fluid infusions one right after the other, along with blood pressure medications, sedation, and other treatments. She gained 10 pounds over night due to the fluid she was given in those few hours. That evening was the first time I met two very important people in Katie's life: Dr. Robin and Dr. Priscila. These women, who were filled with expertise as well as compassion, would be her oncologists for the next six months. These women would walk us through Katie's worst fear. And mine.

I was truly relieved to be in Cincinnati. I was grateful for Dr. Robin and Dr. Priscila. I was hopeful to begin a new treatment plan. I was even trying to live above my circumstances. But I was filled with questions again. And doubts. *How do I find peace? How do I rejoice in this? Can I really live above these circumstances? How do I find the strength of God's life in me when my little girl can't even breathe? And by the way, God, where are you?*

◁

Katie

You were taught not to live the way you used to. You must get rid of your old way of life. That's because it has been made impure by the desire for things that lead you astray. You were taught to be made new in your thinking. You were taught to start living a new life. It is created to be truly good and holy, just as God is.

— Ephesians 4:22-24 (NIrV)

The Son is the image of the invisible God, the firstborn over all creation.

— Colossians 1:15

What on earth am I here for?

PURPOSE!

One purpose: to reflect the image of God.

Ephesians 4:22-24

Colossians 1:15

Jesus - image of God, ♡ of God, ♡ for people.

Jesus - hung out with outcasts purposefully, cares about ALL people!

Jesus - was poor, HUMBLE.

Jesus is NOT normal.

To look like Jesus, you must know what Jesus looks like.

The way the world sees Jesus is through US!

makin' the best of it . . .

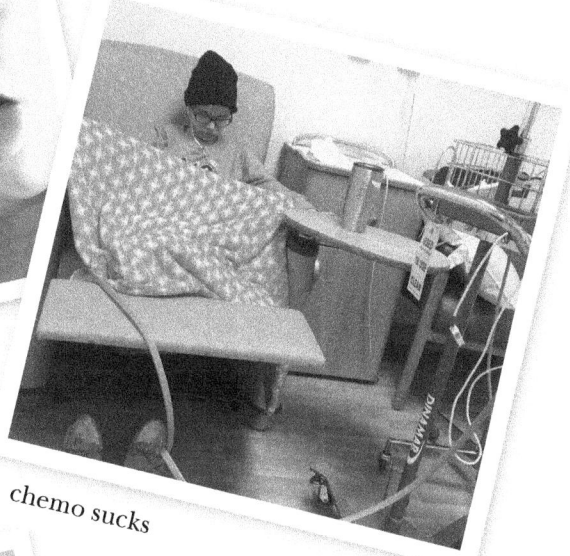
chemo sucks

wouldn't be Christmas without this crazy family! love you guysss, thanks for the chaos!

love my little Sophie ♥

thanks for keeping me smiling :)))

throwback to math homework with the padre

GO MOUNTAINEERS!!!!! ❤

my first friend

Grace VanderWaal wanna
be :)))

here, take some joy :)

I haven't had a time like this in too
long. Thank you ladies so much for
treating me like NORMAL, we need
to do it again!

they left me and I fell on my butt, does
that tell you how good I am? ;))

PART 3

The Relapse

Katie

Let God's light shine in me.

Sarah

On April 19, 2017, while Katie was being flown to Cincinnati Children's Hospital, I was en route in my own vehicle being driven by my long-time friend, Cari. Katie and Ella, Cari's daughter, had been the closest of friends from birth. Quite literally. Ella was born just a few weeks before Katie and they had been in each other's lives ever since. As Cari drove, I alternated between talking frantically due to the adrenaline of the day and resting my eyes quietly due to the exhaustion. Somewhere along the AA highway in Ohio, a helicopter flew directly above us. A medical transport helicopter. Katie's helicopter. I caught my breath as I gazed longingly out the window and then I said, "There goes my hope. My hope is going to Cincinnati." There seemed to be a mere glimmer of light I had not recently experienced, and it was just enough to allow me to remember God was still there. I knew he was there before. Before the diagnosis. Before the relapse. Before the storm that took out all the lights and brought the darkness.

St. John of the Cross refers to *the dark night of the soul.* When we cannot find God in the midst of our current circumstances. I know this place. This place of suffering and pain that cannot be fully explained outside of, perhaps, being referred to as darkness. In the midst of Katie's most intense suffering and, therefore, my most intense darkness, I cried out to God to show himself. On days I drove the long, quiet stretch of road between home and the hospital, I often yelled out through the front windshield, "Show up, God!! Just show up, damn it!!" I imagine the people on the road were taken aback by this woman in the car beside them with the buzz haircut, eyes wide open, screaming and crying while beating the steering wheel, trying to believe that God was still there. "Please just show up!"

Psalm 36:9 says, "In your light we see light." There is so much hope in this one verse. Sometimes, like King David, I cry out that the light around me is becoming dark and what used to be day is becoming night. I feel lost and hidden in this darkness, this pain, this grief, this sadness, this anxiety, this anger, this fear, this anguish, this world. This darkness.

But God reminds me in Psalm 139:11-12 that even the darkness will not be dark to him. Even when I feel encapsulated by it, he will not. For darkness is as light to God, and he makes the night to shine like the day. Consequently, he can still see me even when I can't see anything. And because he is the true light that gives light

(John 1:9), I can have hope. I can find him in the darkness. I can lean into him and his light.

"Though I sit in darkness, the Lord will be my light. Do not gloat over me, my enemy. Though I have fallen, I will rise." Micah 7:8

◁

Katie

Welcome to Thorns and Roses! We are two teenage girls helping other teens just like yourself in their spiritual journey. Our goals are to give teenagers a fun way of learning about God in practical ways and to share our thoughts and experiences with you. Lastly, we want to lead you to Christ even if you're not there yet and give you a boost. Come join us as we make this a fun, spiritual hangout for teens around the world. We're all just roses trying to get rid of our thorns, and we can only do this with God's help. He is with us every step of the way and we are here to make sure you don't give up.

Our blog's mission statement is Matthew 28:19, "Go and make disciples of all nations baptizing them in the name of the Father, the Son, and the Holy Spirit." Throughout this blog that's exactly what we want to do, make disciples of all nations.

Katie came up with the name of the blog, Thorns and Roses, and we're so thankful she did! The best way to explain it is to take a situation you are going through. If you think of just bad and negative things, those would be thorns. We know what it's like to want to talk to somebody about something, but just not know how. We know you've probably heard this a million times, and trust us, so have we, but we really all do go through the same types of struggles. We too, have thought horrible things without wanting or meaning to. We too, have been kept up at night with doubts or fears, but even though these things happen, you can still have joy! We also have roses of life or the amazing and good things in a situation! For example, because we were kept up late worrying, we finally chose to trust in God and have our worries taken away. The decision was made to give our hearts to God. Jesus got thorns all the time but instead of letting them prick Him, He looked to the biggest, prettiest, thorn-less rose of all, God! And Jesus had no pricks on Him.

Our Savior, Jesus Christ, was faced with an incredibly difficult situation. He was being crucified just for saying He was the Messiah. Jesus was innocent! Do you know how easy it would have been for Jesus to just sit there and complain, dwelling in His sorrows? But He didn't. Our Savior endured the cross for us!

God says we all will have struggles and He won't let us go through anything we can't handle. He says that we can strengthen our faith and overcome our struggles by looking to Him. Isn't that amazing? God is always with us just like He was always with Jesus on the cross. He loves us and gives such an amazing grace to all.

Whatever your situation is, we challenge you to find the roses. Look to God, for He is the best rose of all! Rejoice in every square inch of life. We promise there is always a rose.

"Trust in the Lord with all your heart and do not lean on your own understanding. In all your ways acknowledge Him, and He will make your paths straight." Proverbs 3:5-6

-Katie and Maddie

Thorns and Roses

https://tthornsandrroses.wixsite.com/thornsandroses

Sarah

About a week before her original diagnosis, we had accompanied Katie onto the volleyball court before the final home game of the season. The coaches introduced and honored each of the eighth-grade players as their families escorted them. The typical introduction included names of parents, number of siblings, other activities participated in, as well as plans for the future. They read Katie's introduction just as she wrote it: "Katie hopes to become either a teacher or a pastor."

A few months later, while she was still undergoing chemotherapy, Katie decided to start a blog with her friend, Maddie. The purpose of the blog was to encourage teens in their journey with God. She and Maddie set out to write posts that connected Scripture to relevant issues in their own lives. Katie dedicated a journal to this where she recorded Scripture and thoughts as she brainstormed ideas for future posts. She invited Chad and me to read her writings and give feedback. One evening, as she sat on the couch with her Bible and journal open, working on some edits Chad had suggested, she looked up said, "I think I do want to be a pastor. Because I love taking Scripture and helping it make sense to others."

Wow. I loved that. I loved Katie's heart for God and for others. As such, it spurred some of the biggest fights I had with God after her death. In his sovereignty, why would he remove a girl like that from this world? What sense did it make to eliminate her influence on the lives of those around her? She had so much potential for the kingdom of God and, according to my calculations, could have affected many people throughout the course of her life on earth.

God and I discussed this a lot. To be honest, I'm not sure it was a true discussion because it was mostly me yelling at him. And I struggled with it for a long time, both before her death and after. One night, my tears again accompanied the words, "But what about her potential for your kingdom, God? Why would you take that away?" In that moment, I felt a very clear and stern voice say in response: *My Son had more of an impact for my Kingdom after his death than before. So what makes you think I can't do that with your daughter?*

I conceded. My question was answered. The tears continued to roll but the question was answered. Katie had a deep desire to help others learn about God in a practical way and to lead them to Christ. That is what her blog was about. That is what her life was about. And perhaps that is what her death was about.

◁

Katie

Genesis 45:4-8

Parallel truths can seem to be in conflict with each other but actually have a purpose.

Did God tell the brothers to sell Joseph? No.

Did God send Joseph to Egypt? Yes.

SOVEREIGNTY OF GOD

Believe in His sovereignty! Be active and look for the good in the pain. Give it time. You may not know fully or completely understand in this world, on this side of heaven. Just trust.

Do you trust him in ULTIMATE CONTROL?

John 3:16-17

Then Joseph said to his brothers, "Come close to me." When they had done so, he said, "I am your brother Joseph, the one you sold into Egypt! And now, do not be distressed and do not be angry with yourselves for selling me here, because it was to save lives that God sent me ahead of you. For two years now there has been famine in the land, and for the next five years there will be no plowing and reaping. But God sent me ahead of you to preserve for you a remnant on earth and to save your lives by a great deliverance. "So then, it was not you who sent me here, but God.

— Genesis 45:4-8

For God so loved the world that he gave his one and only Son, that whoever believes in him shall not perish but have eternal life. For God did not send his Son into the world to condemn the world, but to save the world through him.

— John 3:16-17

Sarah

I may say I believe that God is sovereign. But do I? Do I really trust him with ULTIMATE CONTROL? Not just with my life but with my children's lives? Katie wrote that parallel truths can appear conflictual to us but can actually be purposeful to God. In Genesis 45, Joseph's brothers sold him as a slave to an Egyptian. But didn't God love Joseph? And if that was true, how could God allow something so horrible to happen to him? Yet, somehow, Joseph is later able to say, "You intended it to harm me, but God intended it for good" (Genesis 50:20). I knew God loved Katie. I knew she was his daughter and that he had a purpose for her life. But she was so sick and her cancer was so ferocious. How could I trust God with that? Could I let go of my control over her life?

Truth is, I like to be in control. I like it when life ensues the way I plan. And most days, that's how it rolls. I put it on the calendar, and it happens. I am the alarm clock. I say when we stay, when we go, and when we eat. I manage the menu, the store list, the schedules, the chore list, the routines, some facilities, many of the purchases and parts of the budget. I refer to my role in the Cobb 7 as Chief of Operations. So, it was very difficult when that role was taken from me. Very difficult.

When Katie was flown to Cincinnati, I could not think clearly. I hate not being able to think clearly. A friend asked if she could help with the kids, so I gave her contact numbers and she initiated a schedule at my house. I looked at another friend and said, "I need to be in Cincinnati when Katie arrives. Chad needs to stay in Charleston until she leaves. We only want to have one of our vehicles there. Please figure that out and make it happen because I can't." He did, and I just followed what he suggested. For the following months, not only did I watch helplessly as Katie fought this horrid disease, but I also listened helplessly to the needs of my kids at home. Friends signed permission slips and sent in field trip money. Neighbors mowed our grass. Family tucked my kids in at night. Dinner just showed up most days of the week at my house. There was almost nothing I could do about any of it from the position I was in.

One of the ways people blessed us during that time was through grocery shopping. My normal mode of operation is to keep a running store list on the refrigerator at home, so my kids continued that practice and each weekend the list was collected and the groceries were delivered. As one friend unloaded boxes of sugar-laden breakfast foods and Little Debbie snack cakes, she told me, "I got everything on the list although I'm pretty sure it is not what you normally buy." Whatever. As long as they ate, I did not care at that point, and I was super grateful for the way others cared for my family in my absence.

One particular weekend, however, I broke. The significance of my lack of control struck me as I arrived home for a couple days and opened the refrigerator to see a tub of butter. A great big tub of Blue Bonnet butter—graciously purchased by someone who loved us. But all I could think was… *that's not even the kind of butter I buy.* As I collapsed into a heap of tears on my kitchen floor, I realized I had lost complete control of my life. I could not protect my kids, sleep in my own bed, manage my house, pursue my career, encourage my husband, mow my grass, or even buy my own butter.

The sovereignty of God is so hard for our human selves. It is hard to understand from our perspective in this world, and it is hard to accept when we don't understand. *God, you be sovereign over the "big things," and I'll be sovereign over everything else—like my butter and my house and my kids and, well, most of my life.* That's not what I say, but sometimes that's how I live. At least, that's how I lived until I couldn't. Until I physically, emotionally, and mentally could not control anything any longer. Until I picked my ugly-crying, can't-hold-it-together-anymore, exhausted-self up off the floor and tapped out. *That's it, God. I'm done. I can't do it. I won't fight you for the position anymore. I'll let go. You be God. I'm out.*

◁

Katie

You are

LOVED

ACCEPTED

A CHILD OF GOD

JOINT HEIR WITH CHRIST

MEMBER OF HIS BODY

SAINT

REDEEMED AND FORGIVEN

COMPLETE

FREE FROM CONDEMNATION

A NEW CREATION

CHOSEN OF GOD

HOLY AND DEARLY LOVED

YOU ARE GOD'S WORKMANSHIP!

Sarah

"For we are God's workmanship, created in Christ Jesus for good works, which God prepared beforehand, that we should walk in them." Ephesians 2:10 (ESV)

I remember sitting on my bed with six-year-old Katie, explaining this verse. "God planned you, Katie. He has big things for you in this life—good works—that he has already prepared for you to do. You won't always live here with Daddy and me." At this, her jaw dropped as if she thought I was kicking her out of the house, and I am not sure how much more she heard me say, but I went on. "And my job, as your mom, is to help you find your way. Not only do I have to teach you how to cook and do laundry and make your own decisions, but I want to help you know who you are in Jesus because you won't always live here with me. In a few years, you will leave home, and I want you to do be confident in who God created you to be because he created you for a purpose."

Before she was diagnosed, Katie had worn a minimal amount of makeup. At thirteen, she had very few flaws to conceal. But as we prepared for her hair loss, I gave her permission to broaden her use of makeup as a way of shifting attention—both for her and for others—away from her head and toward her face. We invited a college friend to share her incredible makeup skills with us one afternoon which led to Katie developing her own fine eye for cosmetics. This brought her a lot of pleasure and she became quite adept at styles that enhanced her natural beauty.

Unfortunately, when chemotherapy medications affect hair follicles, no hair follicles are spared. So, when Katie lost her hair, she eventually also lost her eyebrows and eyelashes. What a difference lashes and brows make in a person's appearance! She looked much more ill without lashes and brows, and she hated it. Which is why she enjoyed the makeup. Lots of days Katie stayed in fleece pajama pants and slippers. No makeup, no big deal. But if she was headed out to see friends, you can be sure she enjoyed dressing up that face.

Our college friend could pencil some very realistic hair growth onto a face (one time she drew a beard on Annie that looked like puberty had struck in an odd way), and Katie learned from her how to pencil in perfect little eyebrows. The eyelashes were a bit more challenging, though, and when hers became sparse, we bought some false lashes to try. Having never applied false eyelashes before, we were both impressed when we properly positioned them on the (almost) first attempt! We soon learned, however, that applying fake eyelashes over existing lashes is much easier than placing them on naked eyelids. It didn't take long for her lashes to completely disappear, and that made getting those eyelashes on so much more difficult. Sometimes she could do it herself, and some days we worked together for a long time, becoming increasingly frustrated with those tiny hairs and that little bottle of glue.

One day, shortly after she had started wearing the "falsies," she had to leave the house early to go on a winter tubing trip (yes, I know, crazy mom, but I told you I wasn't about to let her miss out on life). I was still in bed when she left early that morning with Chad. When she arrived home late that night and I saw her makeup in place, I asked her how it had went getting the false eyelashes on by herself. She said, "Daddy put them on." Oh, my heart. Yes. "Wow, he did a great job," I said as I hugged her.

After a long day out, or if the lashes were just irritating her for some reason, she took them off in the car on the way home and just stuck them anywhere. Admittedly, I fussed at her occasionally for it. But for many months, in the console of my car, there laid a plastic container of gum with fake eyelashes stuck to the top. It makes me smile as I remember her sighing deeply in the seat beside me, ripping that thing off her eyelid and looking for a place to attach it.

Deep in her heart, I think Katie knew that God created a work of art when he made her—lashes or not, long hair or none. Her confidence in who she was created to be is evident in her writings and her relationships. I think she also knew that she was fully loved and accepted for who she was—not only by God but also by her friends—and, as long as she knew that, a little bit of makeup was perfectly fine. Katie was undoubtedly God's workmanship, and she was undoubtedly created for a purpose.

◁

Katie

> We demolish arguments and every pretension that sets itself up against the knowledge of God, and we take captive every thought to make it obedient to Christ.
>
> — 2 Corinthians 10:5

> You will keep in perfect peace those whose minds are steadfast, because they trust in you.
>
> — Isaiah 26:3

focus on God

God has gifted me with AMAZING freedom, including the ability to choose the focal point of my mind.

CHOOSE GOD

Make your goal to bring every thought captive to HIS presence.

When your mind wanders, lasso it.

His light will cause anxious thoughts to shrink and shrivel.

Judgmental thoughts are unmasked.

God will guard me and keep me in unconditional peace as I keep my focus on Him.

2 Corinthians 10:5

Isaiah 26:3

Sarah

I have so many memories of Room A568 at Cincinnati Children's Hospital. It was our home for several months. Katie, Chad and I lived out of a few drawers and four cabinets in that room. A few shirts and pants, toiletries, something to read, and a few snacks. That was it. It is kind of incredible how simple life can become at times.

The room was about the size of an average hospital room. In addition to Katie's bed and equipment, there was a small desk and chair, a reclining chair, and an oversized plastic chair in the corner by the window. The reclining chair took up too much space in the room, so we stowed it in the bathroom during the day. We rolled it out when it was time to shower and then pushed it back in after we finished. The plastic chair was wide enough for Chad and me to both sit in, albeit closely. This same chair converted into a bed roughly the width of an oversized twin mattress. Every night we pulled out that chair and made our bed. We added an egg crate foam pad which provided a good deal of extra comfort, covered it with a sheet, topped it with a blanket from home, and tucked ourselves in. Chad and I usually slept there together. When one laid on his or her back, the other had to lay on their side. Sometime during the night, we switched positions so each could sleep as comfortably as possible. Throughout the night, whenever Katie cried out for something, perhaps needing assistance going to the bathroom or getting comfortable in bed, we took turns getting up and down with her.

Katie had a lot of difficulty sleeping in the hospital. There were so many factors. Obviously, she was not in her own room or bed. She was at times limited by IV equipment, a chest tube, or oxygen tubing. She was often feverish or coughing or receiving a diuretic which forced her up to the toilet multiple times. Frequently, she was attached to a cardiac monitor which meant wires and alarms. Her medications were due at all hours and her vital signs were necessarily observed. Sleep was difficult for her even when she was exhausted.

After a few weeks of struggling through bedtime, we began to develop a better plan. When the night nurse arrived and began her assessment and plan for the shift, I said, "Okay, let's talk about her care for tonight." We discussed how to consolidate the necessary interventions so that Katie could get as much sleep as possible. I also told the nurse, "Do not do anything to Katie without waking me first." This enabled me to remain an advocate for her at all times. We asked that the monitor be turned off at the bedside so the alarming and lights did not keep her awake. We pulled the curtain in front of the door so the light from the hall did not flood the room each time the door opened. In the morning, we kept the lights off and the blinds closed, allowing her to sleep as long as possible and to recover some of the rest she lost throughout the night.

We also found a routine that seemed to help shrink Katie's anxious thoughts in preparation for sleep. Either Chad or I sat on the bottom of her bed and read aloud to her. Katie was not reading much on her own at the time, so we picked up where she had left off, learning the characters and storylines in the *Christy Miller* book series (which certainly qualified as a "nighttime book" by Katie's standards). That simple act made a big difference in allowing her to relax her mind and capture her restless thoughts. For Chad and me, it gave us another chance to really connect with her outside of caring for her physically. Each night, after we finished reading, one of us prayed aloud as we turned off the lights in A568. The room was dark then, but our hearts and minds were not. God's light was present and focusing on God's light brought peace. And a bit of rest.

◁

Katie

Our universe SPEAKS of God. "The heavens declare the glory of God." Psalm 19:1

"To whom then will you compare God?" Isaiah 40:18

"You are God!" Psalm 90:2

"The number of His years is unsearchable." Job 36:26

The "eternal God." Romans 16:26

Inventor of time. Psalm 74:16

★ always been here and always will be here ♡ ★

"Holy, holy, holy is the Lord of hosts". Isaiah 6:3

He knows every smile and every tear.

"I am God and there is NONE like me." Isaiah 46:9

I can't maintain a holy thought for 2 minutes. If God didn't love us SO MUCH, then I would be terrified.

"If God is for us, then who can be against us?" Romans 8:31

The one who formed me, pulls for me.

His arms are around me. Trust. Believe.

ITS GOING TO BE OKAY ☺

The heavens declare the glory of God; the skies proclaim the work of his hands.

— Psalm 19:1

Before the mountains were born or you brought forth the whole world, from everlasting to everlasting you are God.

— Psalm 90:2

The day is yours, and yours also the night; you established the sun and moon.

— Psalm 74:16

What, then, shall we say in response to these things? If God is for us, who can be against us?

— Romans 8:31

Sarah

We decided Room A568 was the best room on the oncology unit because it had the best window view. Most of the rooms with windows faced the brick wall of another building in the hospital, but this one opened up to the sun. If you looked closely in one direction, you could see the top of one of the animal enclosures at the zoo. If you leaned to the right side of the window and looked back to the left, you could see the top of the outdoor playground on that level of the hospital. The view was certainly better than many of the other rooms. But the best part was the sunsets.

Sunsets are one of the beautiful ways our universe SPEAKS of God. They remind us of his power to create and maintain a world much bigger than our own. They declare his glory and his incomparableness. A sunset is a gift from God we often take for granted—except when you are contained in a single room for weeks at a time. Every day without rainclouds brought a sunset to room A568. The sunsets became glimpses of life outside those four walls. Of light beyond this moment in time. Of the graciousness of God. Of hope.

I did not realize at the time that Katie sent a picture of the sunset to one of her friends nearly every evening. Rylee told me that she messaged a verse to Katie every day with no expectation of a reply. She just wanted to be an encouragement to her. And many days Katie's only reply was a picture of the sunset. A picture of what she was focusing on. A picture of her hope that it was going to be okay.

◁

Katie

Jehovah Nissi - the Lord is your banner.

The names of God often arise in hardships.

When your world falls apart, you can:

- give up

- rely on God

We need something to keep us going. Look to the banner!

Exodus 17:8-16

When you feel like giving up, look up for God's strength.

When you feel like giving up, look around for other's strength. Be an Aaron, have an Aaron. We all get tired. Who will hold you up?? Look around.

Trusting God but not doing our part is useless.

TEAM EFFORT. Community.

The Amalekites came and attacked the Israelites at Rephidim. Moses said to Joshua, "Choose some of our men and go out to fight the Amalekites. Tomorrow I will stand on top of the hill with the staff of God in my hands." So Joshua fought the Amalekites as Moses had ordered, and Moses, Aaron and Hur went to the top of the hill. As long as Moses held up his hands, the Israelites were winning, but whenever he lowered his hands, the Amalekites were winning. When Moses' hands grew tired, they took a stone and put it under him and he sat on it. Aaron and Hur held his hands up—one on one side, one on the other—so that his hands remained steady till sunset. So Joshua overcame the Amalekite army with the sword. Moses built an altar and called it The Lord is my Banner.

— Exodus 17:8-13,15

Sarah

In the Bible, Jehovah-Nissi is one of the names used for God. Just as Katie mentioned, the name means, "The Lord is my Banner." In Exodus, when the Israelites were becoming discouraged in their battle against the Amalekites, they needed somewhere to look for motivation. They needed encouragement. They needed someone to say, "Keep going! You can do this!" Jehovah-Nissi was the banner to which they looked. But Jehovah-Nissi also used people to bring physical and emotional strength to the fight. Moses had been instructed by God to stand on a hill overlooking the battle and to raise his arms as the Israelites attacked, but as Moses's stamina diminished, so did that of the soldiers. As the soldiers felt like giving up, so did Moses. Where would they find the strength to keep fighting? Moses looked around and saw Aaron and Hur. These two men came alongside Moses, physically stabilizing his body and emotionally supporting his mission. The Israelites looked up and saw Moses, aiming his hands into the air and pointing to God. Jehovah-Nissi was a banner of hope in the midst of their battle.

In the midst of our battles, we can also look around for other's strength. We can find an Aaron and Hur to hold us up. We can look to God as a banner to keep pushing forward. In much the same way, our daily strength for Katie's battle often came from the people physically closest to us—the nurses and staff at the hospital. While we had community and family at home in West Virginia providing support in many ways, often we needed someone to tangibly stand beside us and hold us up. We needed people right where we were, and many of the staff members became our community.

We had several excellent nurses, but two of Katie's favorite nurses were named Megan and Meg. Megan worked night shift and Meg worked day shift. Katie often remarked that it would be great if we could just have the two of them all the time. Night shift Megan sat and played Uno with us when she had a few minutes. She looked at pictures and swapped stories with us. Day shift Meg celebrated with us on the day Katie was discharged and we celebrated with her when she announced her pregnancy. Katie was so excited to take a baby gift to her during one of our trips back to Cincinnati. They wanted her to overcome her disease as much as we did, and they stood with us, bolstering us in many ways. One morning as Katie's bed was pushed through the doors of the operating room for yet another unexpected procedure, I wilted into the arms of the nurse who happened to be standing next to me. She was my support that day. Another morning the strength to push forward came from a nurse who looked me in the eyes and said, "Don't you ever give up hope. No matter what any numbers say, you can always be the one percent. Don't ever give up." These were the people who held us when we were weak and tired.

Various staff members took the time to get to know Katie. They asked questions and paid attention to the answers. They treated Katie as if she was the most important patient there. And although some people connected really well with Katie, others did not. She certainly found a few folks to be a bit annoying, despite the fact that they were helpful and caring. Sometimes their personalities just did not quite mesh with hers, and sometimes she was just too tired and irritated to be kind and engaged. There were days she felt so miserable that she really did not even try to be pleasant, which is completely unlike her. Occasionally, when one of the therapists showed up at her door, she decided she was too tired for therapy that day and tried to get them to give up on her as quickly as possible. When the teacher stopped by to check her progress, Katie sometimes assured her that she and her daddy were planning to do math that very afternoon. As they left the room, she huffed a little under her breath or rolled her eyes. Not everyone was a welcome teammate every day and that's okay.

But it never took long for someone who brought more joy to show up at the door and turn her mood around. Jenna, the child life therapist, often stopped by to say hello or to see if Katie wanted to play a game. Dr. Priscila might sneak in for a few minutes while she made her rounds, showing us a picture of her niece while we shared with her the cherry turnovers from breakfast. Perhaps Molly, our social worker, would smile and wave through the window and then poke her foot through the open door to ask Katie what she thought of her new Converse shoes. These staff members became our friends… our advocates… our tribe. God provided us with the kind of loving community we needed, and they brought strength and encouragement, enabling us to keep going in the midst of the battle.

◁

Katie

Rejoice when it makes no sense.

Philippians 4:4

Don't rejoice FOR all things. Rejoice IN THE MIDST of all things.

Rejoice one square inch at a time. Every square inch provides an opportunity to bring God glory.

Even the most humble offerings of praise are bold declarations of trusting God no matter what.

PRAISE GOD

> Rejoice in the Lord always. I will say it again: Rejoice!
>
> — Philippians 4:4

Sarah

In years past, God, I thanked you for your blessings.

Your faithfulness. Your mercy. Your grace.

Then my daughter, my Katie, was struck with cancer.

And I walked every step with her.

The diagnosis.

The hospitalizations. The chemo.

The hair loss. The sticks and pokes.

The days out of school. The excitement of returning.

The Zofran and EMLA cream always in my purse.

The scans. The relapse.

The weeks of being stuck in one room.

The surgeries. The months away from home.

The games and celebrations we watched from afar.

The friends she missed. The homebound work.

The favorite nurses. The awkward visitors.

The dog.

The residents who invaded our mornings.

The beloved doctors who sat with us.

The ambulance rides. The PICU.

The weakness. The dragging IV pole.

The bedside commode. The medications.

The shower where we both got soaked as I shaved her legs.

The hospital food. The snack machines.

The wheelchair. The trips downstairs to the patio.

The thrill of a day pass. The exuberance of discharge.

The night my family slept under one roof again.

The long day trips. The radiation. The infusions.

The pain. The difficulty breathing.

The suite life. The laughter. The Cone.

The consultations. The questions. The answers that didn't exist.

The anticipation of a wish. The toes in the sand.

The joy.

The disappointment. The frustration.

The fear. The fear. The fear.

The strength.

The hardest words ever.

The last breath.

I was there, God, but where were you?

Where *were* you?

You seemed absent.

No guiding light. No angels. No healing. No miracles.

Just darkness. Quiet darkness.

Yet you *were* there. In the darkness.

Quiet grace. Quiet mercy. Quiet faithfulness.

Sometimes only I could see. Only I could hear.

And only if I listened so carefully.

Your blessings were so very, very quiet.

And my offering of praise was also quiet.

But both were there.

In the darkness,

Boldly declaring their presence.

◁

Katie

"When you hope, be joyful. When you suffer, be patient.
When you pray, be faithful."

This week, we chose a verse out of the book of Romans. I found it in a devotional I was doing titled, 'Fight Back with Joy.' We really felt this verse speak to us, and God also gave us the assurance we needed. As I was writing this out in my journal, there were multiple verses and quotes that went along with Romans 12:12. Then, as I was sharing it with Maddie, Maddie realized she had just read this verse the other day. It was at that point that we both realized these are not just coincidences, they are God-things, and that is how we chose this verse.

To break it up for you, let's start with the first section. "When you hope be joyful..." The word 'hope' means to anticipate or expect. In other words, when you are hoping for something, you are waiting. Waiting is not easy, especially when you're waiting for big news like a job offer or a grade on a test. As you wait, you can make the decision to worry and fret, scared of what's to come. Or you can choose to trust God and have joy. Sometimes it is hard to find something to be joyful about, but you're alive, aren't you? You're reading this off of an expensive electronic, you have meals throughout the day. Paul is saying that in these times of waiting, you can still have joy. Romans 12:1-2 talks about not letting the ways of the world affect who you are. Sometimes when you are waiting, it's easy to just change your ways because you think maybe it'll be easier this way. However, Paul is saying that if you do not conform to this world, then you can see what God wants for you!

The second part of the verse says, "...When you suffer, be patient..." Sometimes the course Christ has charted for us is straight into the storm. We need to learn to trust God in the midst of the storm. We have to know that God won't always take you out of what you are going through but He will never leave you. The trials are only temporary, you will get through this! John 16:33 says, "In this world, you will have troubles. But take heart, I have overcome the world!" Take the example of God being the potter and we are his clay. Do you think it's going to feel good being shaped and molded into a brand new shape? No, it's probably not going to feel good, and it is going to be painful. But just be patient because you are going to be so beautiful when the Potter is finished! God is going to use this situation to change you and mold you into something amazing, you just have to wait a little longer.

The final part of the verse is just as important as the first two. "...When you pray, be faithful." Here it is saying to not forget about God, pray and talk to Him often. 1 Thessalonians 5:17 says, "Never stop praying." I think that one of the main reasons people don't pray as often as they should is that they believe a prayer has to be 5 minutes of formal talking to God. But that's not it! A prayer can be 5 minutes long but it can also be 2 words here and there when something pops in your head. Just think of it as a conversation with your 'Dad'. There is no right or wrong time of day to do it, either. If you struggle with being able to focus, you're not alone! There will always be distractions, but I believe that God has put these here so that you have the discipline to make Him a priority through the distractions. If you are able to have that discipline, then your faith will grow stronger. Also, if you struggle with figuring out what to say to God or how to say it, here are some ideas: Journal, praying psalms, speaking out loud, or even talking to a wall or pillow sometimes helps. Praying shouldn't be nerve-racking like talking to a teacher. It should just be like a normal conversation with your (Heavenly) Dad.

This week, we want to challenge you to find a way to be joyful while you hope or wait. We challenge you to be patient as God is changing you and molding you through your situation. And finally, we challenge you to "never stop praying." When you see a 'God-thing' in your life or something strikes you as amazing, just send a little 'thank you' or 'wow' up to Him. This week whenever you get a chance, we encourage you to listen to 'Joy' by Rend Collective, it is a really good song and we feel that you can connect it to what you read today!

Don't forget to check back in next Friday for another post. We really hope that you got something out of today's blog post. Have an amazing week! God Bless!

Therefore, I urge you, brothers and sisters, in view of God's mercy, to offer your bodies as a living sacrifice, holy and pleasing to God—this is your true and proper worship. Do not conform to the pattern of this world, but be transformed by the renewing of your mind. Then you will be able to test and approve what God's will is—his good, pleasing and perfect will.

— Romans 12:1-2

"I have told you these things, so that in me you may have peace. In this world you will have trouble. But take heart! I have overcome the world."

—John 16:33

... pray continually

— 1 Thessalonians 5:17

Feinberg, Margaret. *Fight Back with Joy.* Lifeway Press, 2014.

Sarah

When Katie's cancer returned, her smile disappeared. Which was really not surprising. It was her worst fear. And from the moment she relapsed, the bad news seemed to flow endlessly. But seeing her depressed was just as hard as seeing her sick because that is not who Katie was. I was becoming increasingly concerned, not only that she may not go home again but also that she may not smile again. Katie's physicians were wonderful and treated her with such compassion, but I felt like they had not had the chance to meet the real Katie—the Katie who loved life and enjoyed people and radiated such light. They had not even seen her smile. Not once. So, one day as I sat in the quiet room at the end of the hallway with Dr. Robin, I pulled up a video on my phone of Katie dancing and smiling and being silly. I told her, "I want you to see who Katie really is because that kid in that room is not my kid. This is my kid. This is my Katie. And I need that Katie back. And I need to take her home to make memories with her siblings. Even if just for a few days."

Any time Katie showed improvement, I begged to take her home for a couple days. Every weekend I hoped she would be well enough to leave for just one night at home in her own room. Dr. Robin assured me how desperately she wanted that for Katie and for us, but she also wanted to be confident Katie could physically tolerate it. I never doubted she was doing everything possible to make that happen and, eventually, she did exactly that. Exactly what I had begged her to do. It required intense radiation, immunotherapy, and anti-depressant medication, but Dr. Robin enabled me to take home my happy, joyful child with the big contagious smile. And that is the Katie who lived at my house for the next three months. That is the Katie who went to an O.A.R. concert with her aunt and uncle, took Daniel to the parade in town, and swam in the neighbor's pool. That is the Katie who played Nertz with her friends, kayaked in the lake with Annie, and read her book on the beach beside me. Even then, every day wasn't good, but it was good enough that Katie could be joyful in hope, patient in suffering, and faithful in prayer.

◁

Katie

I am fearfully and wonderfully made.

The Velveteen Rabbit

Discover beauty and value on the inside.

It's the presence of wear and tear that awakens us to the depths of God's fierce love for us.

A DEFIANT JOY

Open myself to the joy of being loved and loving others in our brokenness!

Imago Dei. In the image of God.

When you give the gift of being real, you help others see Jesus more clearly and bring comfort and joy.

"He comforts us in all our troubles so that we can comfort others."

Love YOURSELF

Don't WEAR A MASK

Be who you are

> Praise be to the God and Father of our Lord Jesus Christ, the Father of compassion and the God of all comfort, who comforts us in all our troubles, so that we can comfort those in any trouble with the comfort we ourselves receive from God.
>
> — 2 Corinthians 1:3-4

Sarah

Katie had physical therapy (PT) and occupational therapy (OT) a couple times each week while in the hospital. The tasks Katie worked to accomplish during these sessions depended on her physical abilities at the time, and it literally changed from week to week. At first, she was transported to the PT department via wheelchair. Once there, she moved around the room with a bit of assistance and performed some simple exercises. She played the card game Slamwich with the occupational therapist. He often raised the table height, urging her to stand the entire time, sometimes even balancing on one leg and then the other. She progressed to being able to walk to PT, at first using the elevator and then eventually taking the stairs. She rode the stationary bike, watching the screen in front of her as she traversed a path through the forest. Her weakened leg muscles made even the initiation of a forward pedal movement difficult.

She worked hard at all of this, but sometimes she hated it. She hated that her body could not even perform these simple tasks to the degree she would have liked. She did not have the strength or stamina to complete these exercises that would have been so simple for her just a few months earlier. But her muscles were atrophied from lack of activity and her lungs were unable to provide the oxygen she needed for long periods of exertion. The physical therapist always commented about how hard she worked, but Katie wanted to get better more than anything.

One day, when her breathing was particularly stressed, the therapist stopped by to take her to the department for OT. However, because Katie was unable to leave her room or to go off the monitor for any length of time, she decided to bring a TV and game system cart back to Katie's room for therapy that day. Katie was less than enthusiastic about this arrangement, but she finally agreed to play Mario Kart. It was quite funny when the therapist handed her a controller and Katie quickly began setting up the game for them, choosing her character and vehicle and a course for the race. As she quickly assessed Katie's Mario Kart skills, the therapist commented that she was probably not prepared for what she was up against. She encouraged Katie to stand in front of a chair while she played, but even standing made Katie's respirations and heart rate go up so high that she had to finish the game from a seated position. We, of course, teased her that she was getting overly excited about the game which was "obviously" why her monitor continued to alarm. Katie knew as well as we did that wasn't true, but it was a little easier to joke about the game than admit she was unable to stand for more than a minute at a time.

After she was released back to West Virginia, Katie visited a PT clinic once or twice a week to continue building strength and endurance. This girl who loved to jump on trampolines, run for miles, and exercise in her bedroom could now barely sustain a slowly paced walk on the treadmill. She wanted to get stronger and the therapists loved seeing her desire to work hard so she started to push herself more. But I had to tell them no. She couldn't do more; she could only do a little. The lymphoma was putting pressure on the main vessels around her heart and taking up space in her lungs. Her body could not tolerate doing more. It was so incredibly difficult for me to see the physical strain of her small effort, the limits forced upon her by her disease, and the wear and tear on her petite body.

When I reflect on what Katie wrote about the Velveteen Rabbit, I remember that reference in the study we completed together. In the story of the Velveteen Rabbit, the rabbit learns that being deeply loved may lead to patches of hair being rubbed off and joints becoming wobbly and stains becoming visible. But he also learned that being loved like that does not make you ugly, it makes you Real. It makes you aware of the beauty and value on the inside. In the same way, while the wear and tear on Katie's body made her physical brokenness more visible, it also allowed the light of Jesus to be seen more clearly. When she looked beyond her own beauty and strength and abilities, she became more and more aware of the depths of God's fierce love for her.

Katie

John 14:13-14

"In Jesus name"

"For your glory"

Jeremiah 33:2-3

Not about getting the results you hoped for but about bringing more glory to God.

He will do things in & through us that we never thought possible.

Sometimes the things we think are best aren't what God thinks are best.

We don't always understand why we ask for certain things and God doesn't always give them to us.

Psalm 30:11

And I will do whatever you ask in my name, so that the Father may be glorified in the Son. You may ask me for anything in my name, and I will do it.

— John 14:13-14

This is what the Lord says, he who made the earth, the Lord who formed it and established it—the Lord is his name: "Call to me and I will answer you and tell you great and unsearchable things you do not know."

— Jeremiah 33:2-3

You turned my loud crying into dancing.
You removed my clothes of sadness and dressed me with joy.

— Psalm 30:11 (NIrV)

Sarah

It is so difficult to keep moving forward when the plans are not what we want and when the results are not what we hope. Or when we ask repeatedly and work hard and persevere, but God does not give what we think is best. Surely, he wanted Katie to get stronger and to overcome this disease. It seemed impossible to my finite brain that God could want anything else to come from the situation. But sometimes the impossible is what God does in and through us—not for us.

Katie did not want many visitors when she was hospitalized in Cincinnati. She felt terrible, and she hated for anyone to see her like that. She often stated—and, likely, accurately—that no one knew what to say to her, so having visitors only created an awkward situation. And Katie hated awkwardness as much as any of us. I encouraged her to text or FaceTime with her friends, but she avoided it almost entirely. Very few friends or family came to her hospital room, but there were several reasons for this. First, the oncology floor had a strict policy for limiting visitors in order to reduce the risk of infection to these immunocompromised patients. She was only allowed to have 10 different guests every 30 days other than parents and siblings. Second, she spent a lot of time in isolation which meant absolutely no visitors at all. Finally, we were three hours away from most of the people she knew anyhow. Those factors worked in Katie's favor. They gave us excuses to dissuade company when Katie wasn't in a physical or emotional state to see anyone.

But one day, Katie's best friend, Thessa, came with her mom to spend the afternoon with us. Katie was physically stable at the time and this was the first friend she had seen in over a month. They brought watermelon slices and homemade orange Crush ice cream. Jenna, the child life therapist, was so excited to see Katie visiting with a friend that she told Katie she would arrange whatever take-out the two of them wanted to order for lunch. What did Katie choose? Little Caesar's crazy bread. Seriously, I asked? Yep, that was what she wanted. For a few hours, she wanted normal. So, the two girls sat side-by-side in Katie's bed that day, eating cheap pizza and drinking soda, scrolling through Instagram together. Super chill. And if not for the hospital gown and IV pole, almost normal. It wasn't the way she would describe the perfect day with a friend, but it was good. Really good. We were learning to receive gifts from God's hand even when the gifts he gave were not exactly what we asked for.

◁

Katie

The way we talk to ourselves matters.

Our words have the power to kill and give life.

Less hurtful self-talk. More holy soul talk.

Proverbs 18:21

2 Corinthians 10:4-5

Redirect your inner convo to God using the truth of Scripture.

Judges 5:21 - March on with courage, my soul!

Psalm 103:2

Psalm 27:13-14 - Wait for the Lord.

Psalm 42:1 ✗✱

Psalm 94:19

The tongue has the power of life and death, and those who love it will eat its fruit.
— Proverbs 18:21

Praise the Lord, my soul, and forget not all his benefits…
— Psalm 103:2

I remain confident of this: I will see the goodness of the Lord in the land of the living. Wait for the Lord; be strong and take heart and wait for the Lord.
— Psalm 27:13-14

As the deer pants for streams of water, so my soul pants for you, my God.
— Psalm 42:1

When anxiety was great within me, your consolation brought me joy.
— Psalm 94:19

Sarah

For weeks and weeks, Katie dealt with relentless fevers. When a patient on an oncology floor has a fever, he or she must be in isolation in order to protect the other immunocompromised patients—regardless of the fever's causative factor. So, during times of isolation, there was a cart placed outside the room and every person who entered Katie's room had to put on gloves, a gown and a mask. Now, the door to her room had a large glass window with built-in blinds, and we often kept the blinds open during the day in order to feel more a part of the outside world. When she was in isolation, she watched through the window as the various staff members applied their protective garb. She said this at least gave her the chance to see and prepare herself for whoever was going to enter the room because, well, not every personality is easy to get along with—especially when you have been running a fever for most hours of most days for two months. On a few occasions, we were told the isolation requirement had been relinquished but we saw that the cart outside the room had not yet been removed. For that little bit of time, Katie secretly enjoyed watching the visitors methodically put on their gloves and gown and mask even though she knew they were no longer required to do so. She snickered and said, "They don't even have to do that now." But we were never the ones to tell as we attempted to find a bit of amusement in a bad situation.

Isolation precautions are ordered for various reasons. Sometimes it is to protect one patient and oftentimes it is to protect others. The microscopic organisms that cause crippling disease are not potent because of their size but rather because of their abilities. Isolation precautions, therefore, require placement of a physical barrier to prevent mixing the good and the bad in the body. Our hearts and minds can benefit from a barrier as well—something to prevent the good and the bad from mixing in our souls. When we hear hurtful words from others or speak them to ourselves, the negative effects may seem microscopic in the moment but their ability to overcome us is powerful. We create a barrier of defense for our souls when we use the "weapon" of the truth of Scripture to fight off the lies of the world. Just as an immunocompromised patient understands the potential of bugs more than the average person, Katie understood the power and importance of words. The way we talk to ourselves matters because our words have the power to kill or to give life.

◁

Katie

I AM THE TRUE VINE

Is real change possible?

John 15

God disciplines those He loves

He will continue to teach you and show you what you've done wrong until you stop being stubborn.

He loves you too much to just let you continue with stubbornness and sin.

God only takes away what is a loss to keep and a gain to lose.

REMAIN IN JESUS

Connect through his words. Through prayer and communication. Remember his love. Obey his commands. Our obedience leads to lasting joy.

FOLLOW THROUGH!!

STOP STALLING!!

Forge life giving friendships.

"I am the true vine, and my Father is the gardener. He cuts off every branch in me that bears no fruit, while every branch that does bear fruit he prunes so that it will be even more fruitful. You are already clean because of the word I have spoken to you. Remain in me, as I also remain in you. No branch can bear fruit by itself; it must remain in the vine. Neither can you bear fruit unless you remain in me.

— John 15:1-4

As the Father has loved me, so have I loved you. Now remain in my love. If you keep my commands, you will remain in my love, just as I have kept my Father's commands and remain in his love. I have told you this so that my joy may be in you and that your joy may be complete.

— John 15:9-11

Sarah

If we consider God to be the TRUE VINE and the source for true life, then we need methods and people to keep us connected to him so we can grow into a life of real purpose. Life-giving friendships are those that keep us close to God. These are friends who love us too much to let us remain stagnant; they want to see growth in our lives and will come alongside us to make that happen. Some last for years while others are transitory, and they do not all look or act the same. Life-giving friends are invaluable.

Katie had lots of friends, and she definitely had some that were life-giving in the way they loved her. She had one friend, however, who was different from all the rest. Chevy was Katie's best friend for a season. Someone who showed up when life was at its worst. When I had not seen her smile in weeks, this lovable golden retriever jumped onto her bed and brought back her smile.

At their first meeting, he peed in the hallway. She walked out of her hospital room on weak and unsteady legs to sit in a chair and throw a ball to him. Katie's eyes got as big as her smile and we all just laughed when he hiked that leg up! (Please note—he doesn't normally do that, but Chevy works 40 hours each week and it had been a long day for the pup!) With his naturally crimped ears and snazzy bowtie, he was quite the charmer. I swear that dog could even smile!

Chevy introduced Katie to the outdoor playground on the 5th floor because best friends share secrets. She taught him tricks and gave him treats because, well, friends do that, too. He visited her in the PICU even though it was not in his usual rounds. On hard days when there really were no words to share, Chevy just laid there, because sometimes friends don't have to talk. But he also showed up to celebrate when life was good—like the day she was discharged from the hospital.

He sent encouraging notes when she was going through outpatient radiation. What Chevy was not able to do with his own two paws, his handler managed for him. His handler is a child life therapist, also named Katie, who loved on our family in ways that went well beyond whatever paycheck she received. She knew our Katie's personality, what she liked, what upset her, how to help her through procedures, her favorite foods, what staff she related to best and who she enjoyed the least.

Chevy spent time with Katie at least a couple times each week. He laid in bed with her on her very last day. He was sitting beside my kids in the little conference room when Chad and I told them their sister was going to die. Having him there was nothing less than God's quiet, beautiful grace. I knew pet therapy existed before we went to Cincinnati, but I honestly had no idea how valuable it could be in a child's healing.

When no doctor, no nurse, no radiation, no modern medicine could heal Katie, Chevy could do what no one else could. He could just be with her. And be her friend.

◁

Katie

> Jesus Christ is the same yesterday and today and forever.
>
> — Hebrews 13:8

Hebrews 13:8

When faith is tested, you ask WHY?

Does God really love me??

He will NEVER leave me!

Same God yesterday when everything was right. Same God today through the toughest trial. Same God forever in future.

FOREVER: He is love, he is good, and he is for us.

Don't base what you think of God on feelings but on truth.

Cling to the truth: He is who he says he is. Forever.

Sarah

Have you ever heard of "playing 'possum?" This is a phrase often used to describe someone who is pretending to be asleep. Opossums will often do this—pretending to be asleep or dead—as a way of defending themselves against predators. Katie learned to "play 'possum" pretty well during her hospitalizations, and she became very good at using this method to protect herself from unwanted interactions. She often knew when she had reached her capacity for dealing with people or answering questions or receiving information. So, she softly closed her eyes, leaned her head to the side, and rested. It took Chad and me a while to realize she was not always asleep just because she appeared to be asleep. Through comments she made later, we figured out she had heard conversations we thought she had missed, and even after we knew she occasionally did this, it was still quite difficult for us to determine when she was actually asleep or when she was pretending.

I learned to appreciate Katie's ability to protect herself this way. And sometimes, I wanted to just close my eyes and pretend I couldn't see what was happening either. To put my fingers in my ears and pretend I couldn't hear. To hide under a blanket and pretend I couldn't feel. Most of all, I wanted to pretend I couldn't feel the pain, the heartache and the sense that God had left us. But I didn't need to pretend. I needed to lean into what I know and not what I feel. I know God is love, God is good, and God is for us. I know he is who he says he is. I know he will never leave me. Even when that is not what I feel.

"Where can I go from your Spirit? Where can I flee from your presence? If I go up to the heavens, you are there; if I make my bed in the depths, you are there. If I rise on the wings of the dawn, if I settle on the far side of the sea, even there your hand will guide me, your right hand will hold me fast. If I say, 'Surely the darkness will hide me and the light become night around me,' even the darkness will not be dark to you; the night will shine like the day, for darkness is as light to you." (Psalm 139:7-12)

◁

Katie

Proverbs 3

Don't let love and truth ever leave you. Trust in the Lord with all your heart.

★ You won't always understand.

REMEMBER HIM

Don't be wise in your own eyes.

Respect the Lord ♡

Proverbs 4

Get WISDOM. Get understanding.

Hold onto God's teaching and guard it WELL.

Guard your heart ♡

LOOK STRAIGHT AHEAD

Let love and faithfulness never leave you; bind them around your neck, write them on the tablet of your heart. Trust in the Lord with all your heart and lean not on your own understanding; in all your ways submit to him, and he will make your paths straight. Do not be wise in your own eyes; fear the Lord and shun evil.

— Proverbs 3:3, 5-7

The beginning of wisdom is this: Get wisdom. Though it cost all you have, get understanding.

— Proverbs 4:7

Hold on to instruction, do not let it go; guard it well, for it is your life.

— Proverbs 4:13

Above all else, guard your heart, for everything you do flows from it. Let your eyes look straight ahead; fix your gaze directly before you. Give careful thought to the paths for your feet and be steadfast in all your ways.

— Proverbs 4:23, 25-26

Sarah

Katie hated needles. She dreaded immunizations—and so did the nurses who had to hold her down to give them! She did not like for me to remove a splinter from her skin, and she squealed in fright at the sight of blood. So the needles that came with cancer were not something to which she ever really adjusted. Upon her initial diagnosis, the surgeon placed a port in her chest which allowed the harsh chemo medicine to circulate in a large vessel close to her heart instead of a small vessel in her arm. The good news about the port is that accessing it is relatively easy and not very painful. Katie, however, still hated the thought of that needle going through her skin and she dreaded it every time. During her first round of treatments, she also received an injection every three weeks to boost her immune system. We learned as we went along how to best manage these situations. I stood in a certain place, holding her arm in a certain position, while she clenched my other forearm and left embedded nail marks. It really never got easier for her.

After she relapsed, her anxiety surrounding the port, the needles, and the blood draws increased. The anticipation of it triggered her anxiety but the event itself sent her into a panic. I held her upper body and put my face right next to hers. She fixed her big blue eyes on mine as she yelled, "No, Mommy, no, Mommy, no, Mommy!" I took slow, deep breaths with her. For her. Encouraging her to slow the hyperventilating rhythm that was taking over. When the event was passed, she admitted it was rarely as bad as she had anticipated, yet she was helpless to control her panic. We were both left exhausted, hoping there would be time before the next such occasion.

These moments with Katie were so difficult. The injections and needles and dressing changes were necessary. The agony was not wasted. The purpose was to aid in her healing. Yet it was still incredibly painful for her to experience and tormenting for me to watch. With each procedure, she looked straight ahead into my own tear-filled eyes, trusting me to do what was best for her. In the same way, I looked straight ahead into the tear-filled eyes of God, trusting him to do what was best for us. Proverbs 3:5 says, "Trust in the Lord with all your heart and lean not on your own understanding." A friend helped me see this verse a bit differently when he said, "We are not called to understand; we are called to trust." Admittedly, it is hard for me to trust when I do not understand. It can send me into a panic just like Katie but keeping my eyes on God is the only remedy for this condition.

When Katie improved and was ready to be discharged from Cincinnati, a series of unfortunate events left her without a central line for quick and easy intravenous access. Dr. Robin gave Katie two alternatives. The first option was to have a PICC line placed—a type of IV line that would not require her to be stuck as often with needles—but it would restrict her from swimming and would be visible to others. The second option enabled her to go home without any lines or equipment, but she would have to be stuck for blood and IV access every week or two. It was a difficult decision for her but, since it was summertime and she was all about cute sleeveless shirts and bathing suits, she opted for the frequent needle sticks. In one way that choice was surprising, due to her anxiety with the injection process, but it was not so shocking in another. While Katie was not physically tough, she definitely knew how to look straight ahead and trust in the Lord with all her heart.

◁

Katie

But I trust in your unfailing love; my heart rejoices in your salvation.

— Psalm 13:5

Lord Almighty, blessed is the one who trusts in you

— Psalm 84:12

When I found out I was diagnosed, I felt lost. Then I realized God had a plan, and He still does.

I don't have control over the cancer but I have control over my attitude.

Psalm 13:5

Trust God in the midst of the storm.

JESUS IS MY JOY AND FOUNDATION

* Sometimes the course Christ charts for us is straight into the storm *

Psalm 84:12

Faith is a gift that makes life worth living. Surround yourself with people who fortify your faith in life. In Scripture there were still people living by faith when they died. Even amidst the pain and suffering, God was still at work.

The journey of faith will always take us to places where we need God more.

Only God...

    Can save.

    Can heal.

    Can redeem.

    Can work something good out of this.

The trials are temporary.

FIX YOUR EYES ON GOD

Sarah

The journey of faith will always take us to places where we need God more.

There is this place where I always needed God more. It is a conference room on the 5th floor of the A building at Cincinnati Children's Hospital. I hate that conference room. Every single time we walked in those doors the bad news was dumped on our heads. Spilled in our laps. Splashed in our faces. Every. Single. Time.

Sometimes Katie appeared to be improving with fewer fevers and less shortness of breath. Often, we had just started a new chemo medication. Always the conference followed a CT scan or a PET scan. Chad and I walked in together, smiling and encouraged by our hope that this treatment... this med... this day would bring the report we had been waiting on. And then we walked out, heads hanging low, tear stains on our faces, carrying bad news on our shoes like dog crap that won't wash off, beat up by the words we had just heard. "Why is it always bad news?" I mumbled.

On one occasion, I opened the door to the conference room to see our social worker, Molly, sitting beside Dr. Robin. Hmmm, she had never joined one of our conferences before. On the table in front of her was a small package of tissues. Oh. *This is not going to be good*, I thought. The air left my lungs in a deep sigh, but I tried to cover it with a half-smile and a casual, "Hi, Molly." I remember that being one of the worst days in the 5th floor conference room.

Which conference was the very worst? It is impossible to say. Any given one could have been the worst if they had not progressively worsened one by one. As I reflect on those meetings, I wonder how I even walked out of the room on two legs. I am grateful, however, that God allowed me to hear the depth of compassion in Dr. Robin's voice even as she shared hard words of truth with us. In August 2017, just a few weeks before her 14th birthday, we sat in another small room as Dr. Robin brought up the recent scan results on the monitor. First, she showed us the single area of improvement, and then, she showed us several areas of new disease. That is the day she looked me in the eyes and said, "The Hodgkins will win. I don't know when, but you need to hear me say this: Eventually, the Hodgkins will win." We talked at length that day, and she never hurried to leave us. Then we walked back to Katie's room together. We had been gone so long, and Katie knew something was up. I always allowed Dr. Robin to speak directly to Katie because she had a beautiful way of giving her the truth without destroying her hope. Katie was told both the good news and the bad news that day, but she latched on to the good news and let that buoy her in the midst of the storm.

I think Katie knew how sick she was. She knew that cancer was not going away for her. She knew that from this day forward, her life would be hard. But she never focused on that. It was not that she was naïve or even that she chose to "look at the positive." There was very little positive to focus on. No, Katie fixed her eyes on Jesus and everything else seemed to have less color, less precision, less importance.

◁

Katie

> For I know the plans I have for you," declares the Lord, "plans to prosper you and not to harm you, plans to give you hope and a future.
>
> — Jeremiah 29:11

Jeremiah 29:11

Upset with God. Didn't understand. WHY NOW?

It's all part of God's plan.

★ Maybe I went through this to learn that God knows what's best for me better than I do ★

NOTHING compared to God

Only way for us to know our purpose is to know God's Word.

ARE YOU WILLING TO LEARN?

Sarah

Occasionally, throughout the course of Katie's illness, I put my arms around her and said, "I'm sorry. I am just so, so sorry you have to do this."

Sometimes, when I was walking through the halls of the hospital with my head hanging low against my chest, I sensed God's arm around my shoulders in much the same way. And I heard him saying to me, "I am sorry. I am just so, so sorry you have to do this."

Jeremiah 29:11 reminds me that God knows the plan he has for us. For Katie. He has plans to give her a future and a hope. Plans to prosper her and not to bring her harm.

When Jeremiah shared these words of God with the Israelites, they were in exile in Babylon. The verse immediately prior to this says, "When seventy years are completed… I will come to you and fulfill my gracious promise." Seventy years. Who will be alive in 70 years? Not the ones who heard the words *future… hope… prosper… no harm.* This promise is not about today. It is not about me or Katie. It is not about all the good things I want to happen to us and all the bad things I don't want to happen to us.

God is bigger than that. He sees bigger than that. He wants things for us that are bigger than that.

And he knows that when I begin to grasp some of that 'bigness,' and see beyond my own hopes and dreams for today, then I will call upon him and come and pray to him and he will hear me. I will seek him and find him when I can seek him with all my heart (Jeremiah 29:12-13).

But the key to verse 11 is in verse 14, where God promises to "bring [the Israelites] back to the place from which I carried you into exile." They will go back to their place of hope, the future they wanted. They will go full circle. And so will we. So will I. So will Katie. God will bring her back to himself.

The most beautiful part of this passage is that the word *prosper* in verse 11 is translated from the Hebrew word *shalom.* Shalom. My favorite word. My favorite concept. Shalom means completeness… peace… as it was meant to be.

God does not have plans to harm us, but to give us hope beyond today. And beyond tomorrow. Through all the paths we walk in this life on this earth—many of which are not what we want or even what we hope for—he plans to bring us back to the place we started. Back to himself. Back to Shalom.

It's all part of God's plan, and his plans are for Shalom.

Katie

Galatians 1:10

"Am I now trying to get people to think well of me? Or do I want God to think well of me? Am I trying to please people? If I were, then I would not be serving God."

As a typical human, we encounter different situations every day that make us have to decide who we are going to please, God or the world? As a Christian, however, we know the obvious answer is God. But even though the answer may be obvious, it is definitely not always the easiest. One of the most prevalent problems we face as Christians is the longing to be accepted by the world. We try to fit in and look like everyone else; we want to be popular.

But God calls us to be changed, or as stated in Romans 12:1-2, to be transformed so that we may know what God's will is for us. In other words, be different! I know, for me, this is not always easy. You get weird stares and people start noticing that you're not like them. But is that such a bad thing? People will only remember the smartest, the prettiest, the most athletic for a few years. They will remember the one who stayed pure, the one who always talked about God, the one who made an impact., So leave a legacy. Leave the label of being a Jesus-freak.

This is definitely easier said than done. Matthew 7:13-14 says, "The gate is large and the road is wide that leads to ruin. Many people go that way. But the gate is small and the road is narrow that leads to life. Only a few people will find it." I challenge you to choose the road that pleases God, not the road that pleases man. This will probably take you out of your comfort zone, but when you walk with God it usually isn't an everyday, simple stroll.

A people-pleaser is the opposite. They choose to walk with man instead of their Heavenly Father. They want to make everyone around them happy at all times and will do almost anything to keep it that way. We will lose ourselves in trying to please everyone else. But why does it matter what they think? This is the mindset of an earthly thinker. As Christians, we need the mindset of eternal thinking.

A God-pleaser is someone who aims to please the Lord Almighty. Pleasing God does not mean dressing nice. It does not mean straight A's. It does not mean first place in a track meet. Pleasing God means...

- putting your faith and trust in Him

Hebrews 11:6

- giving Him complete control

Proverbs 16:1

- walking with God, not racing against Him

Micah 4:5

- keeping His commandments

1 John 3:22

- being in the world, not of it

John 17:15-16

- forgiving and showing grace, just as Jesus did

Luke 17:3-4

- don't worry, God will always provide

Matthew 6:25-33

Choosing to please God or to please man is a decision we have to make. You cannot walk with God and walk with man. It is either black or white, there is no gray. I encourage you to give God control. Walk the walk...with the Lord. It can be scary sometimes, but He will never let go of your hand. This week, there is no specific song. However, I do encourage you to turn on your local Christian radio station. This is a way to worship God and it is so pleasing to Him! I also want to challenge you to wear the label of a Jesus-freak and wear it proudly. That is who you are.

To humans belong the plans of the heart, but from the Lord comes the proper answer of the tongue.

— Proverbs 16:1

All the nations may walk in the name of their gods, but we will walk in the name of the Lord our God for ever and ever.

— Micah 4:5

Dear friends, if our hearts do not condemn us, we have confidence before God and receive from him anything we ask, because we keep his commands and do what pleases him.

— 1 John 3:21-22

My prayer is not that you take them out of the world but that you protect them from the evil one. They are not of the world, even as I am not of it.

— John 17:15-16

Sarah

A lthough the role of a hospital staff is to care for the patients, sometimes it felt as if Katie—as a patient—spent a lot of her energy caring for the staff through behaviors such as answering questions, being polite, and pleasing the myriad of people who visited her room. At times, it seemed that someone was coming in that door every 15 minutes. Just as one staff person left, another entered. Physicians, fellows, residents, nurses, physical therapists, occupational therapists, music therapists, massage therapists, teachers, pharmacists, social workers, case managers, hematology, oncology, surgery, anesthesia, on and on and on. And even though we really appreciated all of them, sometimes she (and we) just needed a break from it all. So, Jenna suggested that Katie make a schedule to post outside the door in order to give her some control over her time.

The schedule went something like this: Chevy and his handler came on Tuesdays and Thursdays. Physical therapy was in the early afternoon on Monday, Wednesday and Friday. Occupational therapy generally followed physical therapy. Music therapy annoyed her (even though she loved music) so we kept that one to a minimum. But 4 o'clock to 5 o'clock was blocked out every day for *The Ellen Show.* No one interrupted that time unless they were planning to simply sit and watch Ellen with her. Various people came to her room, looked at the posted schedule along with their watch, and then continued down the hall. Katie loved it. Sometimes she completely ignored their faces peeking through the glass. Sometimes she smirked as they walked away from her door. Peace and quiet. A little bit of *leave me alone* in a world of interruptions. A scheduled time to *not* be a people pleaser.

Katie really enjoyed Ellen and the laughter she brought to the day. She loved the guests Ellen interviewed and the games they played. She always teased me about my lack of knowledge of pop culture and said I would never make it on the show. She got so excited when the guests won something big or when Ellen gave a generous check to a worthy individual or the charity they supported. When she was stuck in her hospital room in Cincinnati, *The Ellen Show* was a little break from Katie's reality every day at 4 o'clock. It was an hour of escape, smiles, and amusement. After all, even Solomon said, "A cheerful heart is good medicine" (Proverbs 17:22).

◁

Katie

These questions Katie answered for an assignment give a bit of fun insight into her personality.

What are you afraid people see when they look at you?

When people look at me, I am afraid they only see a cancer patient. They see someone who needs pity and sympathy. They see someone who misses lots of school. I am afraid they immediately see someone who always wears a ball cap. I worry they miss out on the real me. The me who is just a freshman, a fun friend to have around. I am afraid they cannot see past my sickness, but it does not define who I am!

What's the best thing you got from your parents?

The best thing that I have received from my parents is my family. They have given me four other siblings that I am forever thankful for. It is a constant roommate, playmate, and friend. My parents have given me the best family anyone could ask for!

If you could have a never-ending candle that smelled like anything you wanted, what fragrance would you want it to be?

If I could have a never-ending candle that smelled like anything I wanted, I would choose Bath and Body Works' Stress Relief scent. It is the eucalyptus spearmint and by far my favorite scent ever. Not only is it just a wonderful smell, but it relaxes you and truly is a stress reliever.

What do you like most about your family?

What I like most about my family is how close we are. I have a wonderful relationship with each of my family members. We eat dinner together, as a whole family, at least 3-4 times a week. On Sundays, we attend church as a family. My family means the world to me and I love how woven together we are.

What small gesture from a stranger made a big impact on you?

A small gesture from a stranger that made a big impact on me occurred in King's Island. We were listening to a little band play and a worker, who was a complete stranger to me, walked up and simply stated, "You look really cute today. I love your outfit." It was those nine simple words that just made my day. It was easily the highlight of my week. I had very recently been released from the hospital and was just very self-conscious about a lot of things, especially being out in public. What she said to me left such an impact!

Where would you spend all your time if you could?

If I could, I would spend all of my time lounging on the beach with my friends.

What do you take for granted?

I take for granted so many things in life. One of the biggest things, I believe, would be a loving family. It is all I have known. I have never even considered my parents being separated. My siblings and I have always been together. To me, this just seems like normal. It is what everyone is used to, right? But looking around, having such a loving family is not as common and it breaks my heart to see this. Not only family, but all of the luxuries I have. Day to day, I may even call them necessities. However, they are privileges and not a right. It could be taken from me at any time.

If all jobs had the same pay and hours, what job would you like to have?

If all jobs had the same pay and hours, I would love to just play with puppies. I could do it all day, every day. They just brighten your mood and if I am making good money and working just as long as any other jobs, I mean I can't complain.

What's worth spending more on to get the best?

In my opinion, one small thing that is worth spending more on to get the best would be a drink. I believe it is so worth it to spend ten cents more to get a large versus a small.

What takes up too much of your time?

Social media and texting take up way too much of my time. Other, more important things get pushed out of the way because of this. It is something I really need to work on with my self-control.

What is the most annoying question that people ask you?

The most annoying question that people ask me is, "Are you Katie Cobb?" I get asked this almost every time I go out in public because so many people follow my story.

Sarah

Chad and I have tried to create an atmosphere in our home that invites connectedness in our family. We want our kids to have time to simply be together, and sometimes that means saying no to other opportunities. We try to eat dinner around the table several nights each week and to find ways of enjoying one another. When the kids were small, we had "horsey" races in the living room as Chad and I crawled from one end of the room to the other, each with a child on his or her back. When they got a little bigger, we played football in the side yard until my pregnancy with Daniel forced me into an all-time quarterback role. Although we may have occasionally forced family togetherness through a game of UNO, we never had to beg anyone to join us for ice cream at Dairy Queen. The Cobb 7 was a tight gang, so being separated for several months while Katie was hospitalized was difficult for all of us.

While we were in Cincinnati, our parents and my siblings took turns staying at our house with our kids, attempting to give them as much normalcy in their routine as possible. Chad and I tried to alternate being home and away, but neither of us wanted to leave Katie and we craved the support of one another during that time as well. Sometimes I was gone for more than two weeks at a time, returning only for one or two nights to hug my kids and gather a few items. Our kids asked continually for us to come home. We tried to explain to them that Katie really needed us, but they had a hard time understanding why we could not take turns with them and with her. It was difficult to explain it to them fully because we could hardly explain it to ourselves. We rarely even slept across the street at the Ronald McDonald House because of her fragility.

When we made FaceTime calls to the kids, they cried. And begged. Even our oldest asked, "When are you coming home? Why can't one of you just come home? Why can't you take turns being here and there?" The repeated phrase was, "Please, please come home." It was so arduous to be away from one another and from our usual life.

When I did go home it felt so oddly normal. For brief moments, it was as if we could pretend our reality wasn't reality. I took a shower and slept in my bed and sat on the porch and walked to the park with my kids and almost—almost—forgot. Not that I wanted to forget Katie, but I wanted to forget the nightmare. I liked being home. And I liked not being at the hospital. Sometimes I thought... maybe

I will stay one more night. I'll just leave in the morning instead of this evening. Besides, the other kids need me here for another day. But then Katie called me. And cried. Just like the other kids did a few days before. "When are you coming back?" she asked. If I said, "I think I'll come back tomorrow morning. Is that okay?" she hung her head, caught her tears, and said, "I guess." Oh, I hated it. I loved going home and I hated it, too. I could not possibly be more torn than when I heard my kids all beg for me to both stay with them and return to them.

The following morning, I left to go back to Cincinnati, dropping Daniel off at preschool on my way out of town and knowing I may not see him again for a couple weeks. He had such separation issues after that, and my other kids struggled with similar effects from the trauma of that period. It was an impossible situation, changing everything about the way we did family. We felt at a loss for how to operate in the circumstances. The words of the king in 2 Chronicles 20 rang often in my head: "God, I do not know what to do, but my eyes are on you."

◁

Katie

Genesis 50:20

You INTENDED to harm me, but God INTENDED it for good to ACCOMPLISH what is now being done, the saving of many lives.

There is a higher purpose for the pain. God is a master weaver and a master builder. He can reuse and rebuild the junk in your life into good.

"Look at my blueprint for your life. I can take what you think is trash and make it BEAUTIFUL!" - the Master Builder

★ EVIL RECYCLED FOR GOOD ★

While we wait, God works. These hard times aren't wasted. Wait for the bigger picture. TRUST ♡

Life is FRAGILE. Suffering produces a longing for ETERNITY.

The battle between fear and faith is real and it's hard. Each day presents a choice to celebrate or lament.

We really need COMMUNITY. Not a luxury but an absolute necessity. There is POWER in an encouraging word.

My ultimate source of hope and joy is in CHRIST alone.

Romans 8:1

You intended to harm me, but God intended it for good to accomplish what is now being done, the saving of many lives.

— Genesis 50:20

Therefore, there is now no condemnation for those who are in Christ Jesus, because through Christ Jesus the law of the Spirit who gives life has set you free from the law of sin and death.

— Romans 8:1-2

Sarah

Our friendship with the Bramlee family was born out of adversity. We knew of one another through a few mutual friends. Although we were new to living in this environment, the Bramlee family had a long history of hospitalizations in Cincinnati due to the chronic nature of their child's undiagnosed disease. When Cohen had an appointment at the hospital while we were there, his mother, Carrie, reached out to me to see if we could connect. Oddly enough, when I saw her that evening during dinner at the Ronald McDonald House, my heart immediately recognized her even though we had never met before. Within minutes, our lives began to intertwine.

That day's scheduled appointment turned into a four month long unscheduled hospitalization for Cohen. During that time, Carrie and I learned to lean into one another for support and encouragement because, even with a myriad of friends and family who want to offer support in those circumstances, no one else is physically present, day after day, and no one else quite understands the same as another mom who is sleeping beside her child in a hospital bed every night.

On days when both of our children were *well* enough for us to leave their rooms and *if* we could coordinate a few minutes of calm between their procedures, I met Carrie downstairs and we walked to Starbucks together. To the secret Starbucks.

A hidden little place in a nearby building that was unknown to many, Carrie had learned the way to the secret Starbucks from a bookstore clerk: "Go up the middle elevators, turn right and then turn left, go through the door that goes 'click click.' then follow the smell of coffee." Say what? I definitely had to follow her a few times before I could find my way there alone. We were like two young girls with a secret hideout in the woods, sneaking away from the rest of the world. Despite the darkness framing our eyes and the fatigue pulling down our shoulders, we sipped our drinks as if our lives were completely normal, pretending for a minute that our acquaintance had been made at a fancy gala or at a business dinner or even at the playground. Just not at a children's hospital. The secret little coffee shop was a refuge as we vented and cried and laughed. And limped through our days together.

A few months later, Katie and I returned to Cincinnati for a visit to the outpatient hospital. That day, Katie was receiving an infusion of her immunotherapy medication and a thorough checkup. Her Make-A-Wish trip to Hawaii was quickly approaching, and we had also snuck in some shopping that morning in preparation. Cohen remained hospitalized even then, so Carrie stopped by to visit with us for a few minutes. As she returned to the elevator that afternoon, Carrie physically bumped into a physician with whom she had been attempting to connect in regards to Cohen's case. This "bump" on the elevator led to a long conversation in the hallway which concluded with the physician agreeing to lead the charge on this road to a diagnosis for Cohen. Carrie was astounded with the potential this relationship brought to her son and her family. She immediately ran back to our room and sat down on Katie's bed, giddy with excitement. Looking into Katie's face, she said, "You are my miracle, Katie! Because of you, I met Cohen's new doctor. I just know she is going to be the answer we need for Cohen, and it is because of you! Katie, God is already using you in a big way!" Katie just smiled her big, humble smile, unsure of exactly how her presence could have so much of an impact. But this is how God works and weaves and recycles evil for good. He does not waste anything in our lives.

Carrie hugged Katie and me before returning to her own hospital room. Cohen was soon discharged to home, and that newfound relationship grew into something incredible in the pursuit of his disease and treatment—and that of other children fighting the same unknown enemy. Perhaps God took something intended to harm us and used it for good to accomplish what is now being done, the saving of other lives. After all, he is the Master Weaver.

◁

Katie

The world around me seems to spin faster and faster til everything's a blur.

There is a cushion of calm in the center of my life—where I live in union with God.

I need to return to this center as often as I can.

This is where I am energized—filled with God's love, joy and peace.

The world is a needy place—don't depend on it.

Learn to depend on God alone—my weakness will become saturated with God's power.

Live in the light of God's presence and my light will shine brightly in the lives of others.

Galatians 5:22

1 John 4:12

But the fruit of the Spirit is love, joy, peace, forbearance, kindness, goodness, faithfulness, gentleness and self-control.

— Galatians 5:22-23

No one has ever seen God; but if we love one another, God lives in us and his love is made complete in us.

— 1 John 4:12

Sarah

Katie was a strong, independent child. At thirteen, she should have been growing in her independence even more. Finding her own identity. Managing her own person. It should not have been a time for using a bedside commode. A portable toilet that sits in the middle of the room because the bathroom ten feet away is too far. Too far because the diuretic medicine makes the need to urinate come so quickly. Too far because there is not enough time to get all the IV tubing and heart monitor wires out of the way. Too far because of the shortness of breath that comes with any activity. Ten feet is too far. So, the bedside commode just sits there by the door for everyone to see. The curtain is pulled to give privacy so that maybe *not quite everyone* will see. But the dignity is gone. Long gone.

Even when the bedside commode was not necessary, assistance to the bathroom was. Up and down all day and night, pushing the IV pole, carrying the chest tube, taking off the pulse oximeter, disconnecting the heart monitor. Into the bathroom, situate, and then step outside. Give her a little privacy. Then help to stand, support to walk, and back to bed. She was so weak. Reconnect, reposition, and hopefully return to sleep.

When the chemotherapy medications had been out of Katie's body long enough to allow her leg hairs to grow again, I convinced her that shaving her legs would make her feel much better. On unsteady legs she walked to the shower, but she was unable to navigate the entire process alone, so we both got soaked as I shaved her legs that day.

It was unlike Katie to be so dependent on me, but her weakness necessitated it. And I wanted to assist her in that way and to provide the strength she did not have on her own. It was a blessing to be able to do so. Our dependence on God is quite similar. If we acknowledge our weakness and allow him to come alongside and confer the abilities we do not have on our own, his presence begins to energize us and shine through us in ways we never could have attained alone. And we are both blessed in the process.

♡

Katie

The more you are in a continual state of ASSISTANCE from God and others, the STRONGER you will be. Simply ASK FOR HELP!

Reserve a daily time with God!

Psalm 121:1-2. Know God! Connect with him!

    Time and place. CLAIM IT!

    Plan.

    Pen and paper. WRITE IT DOWN!

    Bible.

    Be consistent.

    Prayer!!

Have an ongoing support team! ↳ can't do life ALONE

Ecclesiastes 4:9-12. Two are better than one!

Cultivate relationships I already have.

Romans 12:9-10. We need help and we need to help others.

Ask and listen.

HOW DO YOU LOVE?

Love well ♡

I lift up my eyes to the mountains—where does my help come from? My help comes from the Lord, the Maker of heaven and earth.

— Psalm 121:1-2

Two are better than one, because they have a good return for their labor: If either of them falls down, one can help the other up. But pity anyone who falls and has no one to help them up.

— Ecclesiastes 4:9-10

Love must be sincere. Hate what is evil; cling to what is good. Be devoted to one another in love. Honor one another above yourselves.

— Romans 12:9-10

Sarah

Katie received frequent care packages in the hospital filled with games and marker sets and notepads and various activities to pass the time. Many of them went unused, however, as she often lacked the physical tolerance or the emotional motivation to do anything stimulating. Like any teenager, she preferred her iPad. She enjoyed playing a few games; Solitaire was her favorite. And she relied on Instagram as her lifeline to all things normal. I often crawled up in bed beside her, adjusting my arm behind her so as to avoid the lines and wires and tubing. She leaned into my chest as I watched over her shoulder. Sometimes I helped her with the next Solitaire move or the next word with friends. Sometimes we looked at silly pins, such as "Bad Tattoos." Sometimes we did a word search together. Sometimes she scrolled through social media posts while I completed a Sudoku puzzle. Sometimes I worked on my computer while she slept, leaning on my shoulder. Curling up in bed with her provided some of the sweetest times. Even when we were not doing anything special.

The year Katie got sick we began following a show on television together called, *This Is Us*. Chad convinced me to watch with him when it first aired, and then Katie joined us shortly thereafter. It was something special we did together on Tuesday nights after the younger kids went to bed. While she was in the hospital, the three of us crawled into her hospital bed to watch. And if Chad or I happened to be home with the other kids, the rule was we could not turn it on until we were all back together. *This is Us* was only viewed when it was us. Together. So, it just makes sense that neither Chad nor I have ever seen another episode since the last time we watched it with Katie, curled up in bed together in the hotel room in Hawaii.

We were each other's support team. Perhaps it appeared that Chad and I were there to give her assistance, but sometimes she did the same for us. We encouraged one another, relied on one another, talked, listened, laughed and loved well. Even when it was so very challenging, we often said it was a blessing to be able to care for her because of the joy she brought to our lives. We needed God and each other during those days and that made us stronger, not weaker. It was a reminder that life was not meant to be lived alone.

◁

Katie

Do you not know that in a
race all the runners run,
but only one gets the prize?
Run in such a way as to get
the prize.

— 1 Corinthians 9:24

1 Corinthians 9:24

the Christian life is like a race

the prize is JESUS

It's WORTH it!!

Don't give up. Trust God.

Sarah

In early June, while Katie alternated between showing signs of improvement and signs of significant deterioration, an image became fixed in my mind. I cannot say if it was a dream or a vision or something else entirely, but one day I experienced a very clear impression of Katie that became a source of peace for me.

In my image, Katie spoke to me from heaven and said, "It's okay, Mom. It was worth it."

It was worth it.

As I watched her that very day struggle to breathe well enough to even walk to the bathroom alone, none of it seemed worth it. The hospital. The chemo. The waking up every morning to fight again. It didn't seem worth the effort. Honestly, sometimes trusting God didn't seem worth it either.

But then God gave me this image of Katie reaching back from eternity, where she stood in joy and a radiant smile, saying, "It's okay, Mom. It was worth it."

I think that was when I knew God was not going to heal Katie. I had begged him to heal her, but he seemed to keep telling me *No*. That day, he took the hope I had for Katie's cancer to be eradicated. But in its place, he gave me hope for her cancer to be exchanged for something more. He gave me hope for redemption. He gave me hope that one day, from Katie's perspective, it would be worth it.

◁

Katie

Psalm 11:4

Everything was fine and normal until one day. I go to the hospital and I stay for 10 days until I get my diagnosis.

I was BROKEN.

WHY????

But God NEVER left my side. As much as it seemed he did.

God was still in control. God is so high up. He can see the big picture. We only see a speck.

DON'T LOSE FAITH

Seek Him! ♡

The Lord is in his holy temple; the Lord is on his heavenly throne. He observes everyone on earth; his eyes examine them.

— Psalm 11:4

Sarah

When Katie was first diagnosed with Hodgkin Lymphoma, she had been in the hospital for nearly 10 days awaiting a final pathology result and treatment plan. Her primary care physician and my friend, Dr. Liz, stopped by to check on her and encourage both of us. She brought goodies for us and helped me wash Katie's hair that morning. As she was leaving, I stood in the hallway and leaned into her shoulder as the tears just rolled. My worst nightmare was unfolding, and I began to realize my role in this was tremendous. I said to my friend, "Liz, I have to get her through this. Not only physically, but also spiritually. Somehow, I have to get her through this with her faith intact. And I don't know if I can do that." She hugged me tight and said, "You can. I know you can."

During those first few months of treatments, while Katie was home from school, I challenged her to complete a Bible study alongside me. It was a study by Margaret Feinberg titled *Fight Back with Joy*. We worked on the study individually and then watched some of the video segments together. It was never anything terribly forced or scheduled, but over the next couple months, we casually discussed different Scripture and questions brought up in the study. It was good for each of us and many of Katie's journal writings came from this time as she encouraged and challenged herself to keep her focus on God during this difficult season.

Months later, in the midst of her relapse, she asked me directly, "Mom, how do you trust God when this just keeps happening?" With a deep breath and a heavy exhale, I answered her, "Katie, I don't fully know. All I know is that when I look back at my life, I see how God has been faithful. And I trust that his character is such that he will continue to be faithful. But I don't pretend to understand it." There was—and is—no magic answer for that question. Not for me, not for her, not for anyone. Maintaining faith in God when nothing seems to be going right is inexplicable, but I know that it is not just one experience that builds a deep faith. Faith grows through a multitude of little and big opportunities to trust God, eventually resulting in a faith that sees from an eternal perspective instead of a temporal one.

After being hospitalized for nearly three months, Katie arrived home from Cincinnati on a Thursday. That Sunday, we went to our own church—together— for the first time in months. I thought she might want to stay away from the crowds

Feinberg, Margaret. *Fight Back with Joy*. Lifeway Press, 2014.

of people. I knew she wanted to be treated normally, without drawing attention to herself, so I watched as she entered. With her hat on her head and her Bible in her hand, she walked in as if she had been there all along. She did not hesitate to take her usual position in the very front row on the right-hand side. Same seat. Same friends. Same Katie. Worshipping Jesus with eyes closed, a little sway, a big smile, a lot of singing. I didn't know if she could do it. But I watched her. She did it. After all that she had been through, she did it. She sought God. She kept her faith. And she fought back with joy.

As I stood there in awe, the words in my heart were, *Thank you, God. Her faith is still intact.* Later that day, I wrote in my journal, "Lord, she has a great desire for you. I pray that you would give her the desires of her heart and pour out blessings on her—both temporal and eternal blessings."

◁

Katie

Romans 5:8

While we were STILL SINNERS.

Meaning of this verse just hit me. We were AWFUL people. Didn't even try to love ♡

But Christ - I said CHRIST - died for YOU and ME!!!

What an amazing love.

God HATES sin. But covered His son with it because of that love ♡

God loves the murderer and the priest. EVERYONE!!!

Those standards should be our GOAL.

We'll never be perfect but we sure can strive to be.

Our duty is to bring GLORY.

Philippians 2:5-8

But God demonstrates his own love for us in this: While we were still sinners, Christ died for us.

— Romans 5:8

In your relationships with one another, have the same mindset as Christ Jesus: Who, being in very nature God, did not consider equality with God something to be used to his own advantage; rather, he made himself nothing by taking the very nature of a servant, being made in human likeness. And being found in appearance as a man, he humbled himself by becoming obedient to death—even death on a cross!

— Philippians 2:5-8

Sarah

When I took Katie to the hospital the very first time for her difficulty breathing, I told her to pack a few things in a bag… just in case. Just in case… we have to be there a while for a CT scan or something. That's what I told her, although I had a sense it would be more than that. She was mad about going to the hospital anyhow, so she grumbled as she threw into her bag some comfy sweatpants, a T-shirt and a book. We did not know it then, but that was the first of many JIC bags. Just In Case.

At first, we did not need a JIC bag (we pronounced it "jick"). Katie did so well with treatments that we never had to stay in the hospital more than the hours allotted for infusions. Later, however, we learned to always pack a JIC bag. Contact case, saline solution, shampoo, and deodorant stayed ready to go in a small bag. Grab a change of clothes, toothbrush, a book, and we were out the door. We could pack for at least a couple days in a matter of minutes. When it was necessary to make a day trip to Cincinnati, driving three hours one way for a clinic visit, blood draws, and infusions before returning home that evening, I would say, "Get your stuff together, Katie, and don't forget to pack your JIC bag." Just in case we had to stay longer than expected. Just in case she was admitted overnight. Just in case the day did not go as smoothly as expected. Just in case.

The JIC bag leads me to wonder: Do I keep God in a bag in the corner of the room just in case? As in… just in case I need a spiritual boost… or just in case I can't figure it out on my own… or just in case I do something really, really bad? Or do I allow his love and his presence to be a substantial part of my every day? The depth of love God showed in allowing his Son, Jesus Christ, to carry my own baseness reveals that he wants to be more than just JIC in my life. He wants to be a constant in my day-to-day. Like Katie wrote… Christ died for you and me. What an amazing love.

◁

Katie

Community

"Katie, wake up!" On the joys of sharing a room with an early riser. She makes sure that it isn't past nine in the morning. At least I don't sleep with the kicker. Waking up early and bruised would not be any fun. However, I can't act like some nights I don't enjoy sharing a room. There may be limited privacy, but you have a roommate, a friend, at all times of the night. I had a bad dream. I look over and feel comforted because I am reassured that I am not alone.

Not only is it sharing a room but sharing a house. There are seven of us and a dog. It is never quiet at our place. It is a flutter of activity. There is fussing and aggravation encircled by hugs and the sense of belonging. Everyone is up in your business, but it is because their care is always accessible. Family can be nosy and loving. They are ever present in your life.

In similar ways, it has been a blessing and a curse having so many people follow my story for the past year. I came home after being gone for two and half months to what seemed like my entire hometown lining the streets. How embarrassing! I wanted to sink deeper and deeper into the seat. But how amazing! All of these people are just overjoyed that I am home. They want to show me how loved I am and that I am not alone in this battle. Congratulations, you have definitely succeeded.

Having such a close-knit community is like a wool blanket. Sometimes, it is the most comforting thing. It warms you from the inside out. Feels like a safety net over you. The blanket is calming. The community covers me. Other times, wool blankets can feel a bit suffocating. You feel trapped, claustrophobic. Constantly having everyone know what feels like everything about me. How do I get out? I am wrapped so tightly.

Community is overwhelming at times, but where would I be without it? I always have someone to turn to at all times. This is my life. It is no secret to anyone. The biggest, strongest team I know. What a love that shows!

Sarah

Katie returned home from her extended hospital stay on June 29, 2017. I had received word that there would be a collection of people at home lining the streets and awaiting her arrival. I knew Katie would not approve of this if she had known ahead of time, so I kept it to myself. I slowed down as I entered our little town and she asked what I was doing. Then, as she began to look around, she saw signs and purple balloons everywhere, held by smiling and waving friends, neighbors and community members. Although the outpouring of support that day was a bit embarrassing to Katie, it also succeeded in revealing to her how loved she was. She had never been alone in her fight and that was comforting to her.

As soon as she arrived home, our little social butterfly wanted to see her friends—as many as possible and as soon as possible! A few stopped by on their own, but Katie started planning a party right away for all the rest. She called it her "Come and see me party." It was a casual get together for anyone to stop by—and numerous people did. Many of her peers from school came, and some were accompanied by their parents who also loved Katie dearly. Several families from church and the neighborhood dropped in for a few minutes. Even though she stood on legs that were thin and frail, everyone was happy to see her home and smiling and walking about.

I watched in awe as the scene unfolded in front of me. Just one week previously, I had witnessed this same girl struggle to walk to the hospital cafeteria. Only a month prior, I had seen her persona wither from lack of interaction with people. Scarcely a few weeks before, I had pleaded with God to give her time with her siblings and time with her friends. And this… this is what I had asked for.

That night, Katie slept in her house, in her bed, in her room and beside her sister. Sure, it was overwhelming at times, but this was her life. The biggest, strongest team she knew. She was definitely not alone.

◁

Katie

God speaks to me from the depths of my being.

Hear Him saying soothing words of peace, assuring me of His love.

Do not listen to voices of accusation - they are not from God.

Let the Spirit take charge of my mind - combing out tangles of deception.

Be transformed by the truth that God lives within me.

Let God's light shine in me

Don't dim it with worries or fears.

Pause before responding to people or situations.

Give God's Spirit room to act through me.

Hasty words and actions leave no room for God.

Romans 8:1-2

Colossians 1:27

1 Cor. 6:19

Therefore, there is now no condemnation for those who are in Christ Jesus, because through Christ Jesus the law of the Spirit who gives life has set you free from the law of sin and death.

— Romans 8:1-2

To them God has chosen to make known among the Gentiles the glorious riches of this mystery, which is Christ in you, the hope of glory.

— Colossians 1:27

Do you not know that your bodies are temples of the Holy Spirit, who is in you, whom you have received from God? You are not your own; you were bought at a price. Therefore, honor God with your bodies.

— 1 Corinthians 6:19-20

love these dudes ♥

be happy :))))

love my fam so much
:)))) ♥

happy dad's day

happy momma's day

PT was rough today

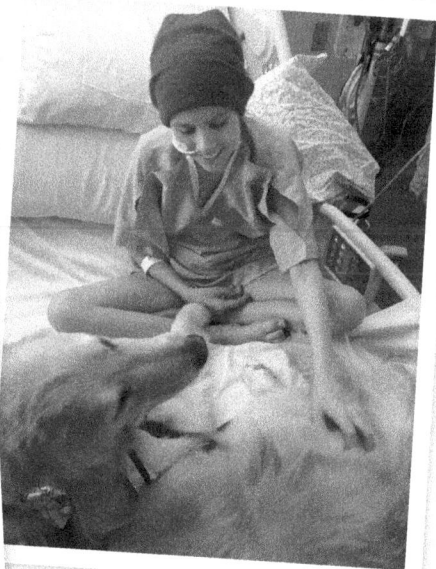
meet Chevy :))))

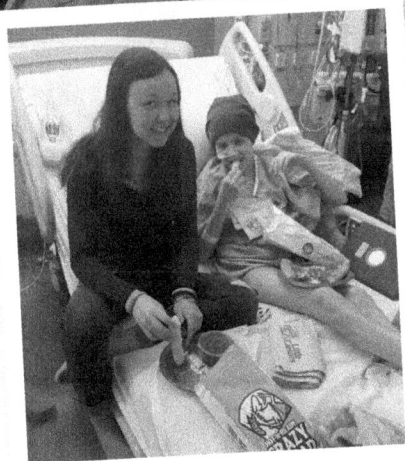
crazy bread, Ellen show and friends...
what else do you need? 💜

sunshine and Chevy

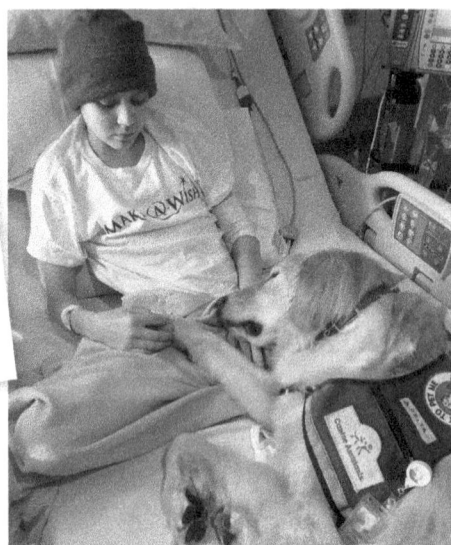
thank you for always being there for me

it's discharge day!!!

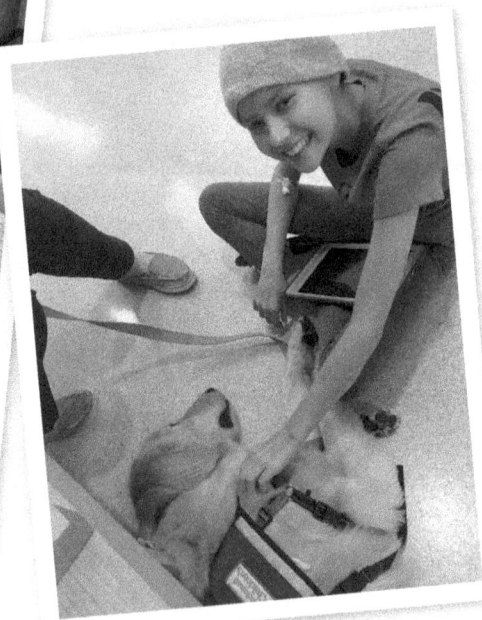
sweet Chevy 🖤

best parents ever 🖤

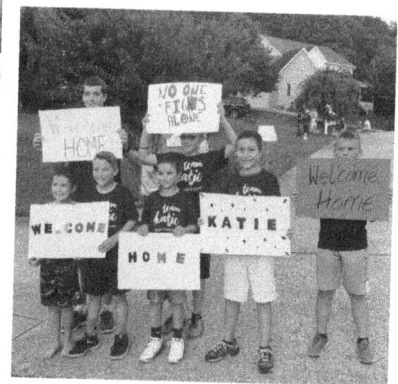

ahhhhh it's so great to finally be home!!! :))))

thanks to everyone who came to hang out with me today. love you all :))))

PART 4

Finally Home

Katie

What I have gone through is no mistake. It is a part of my story.

Sarah

Katie's personality was one of the best parts of her life. One of the best parts of her story. She was full of laughter and enthusiasm for almost anything. Her smile seemed to be an outflow of the light inside her, and it became contagious the moment it spread across her face.

One friend told me the story of when she babysat our kids overnight and Katie helped Daniel—who was recently potty-trained—in the bathroom. Even though Daniel accidentally peed all over Katie's clothes and she had to change her outfit, she smiled the entire time and did not seem to mind the ordeal at all.

Another friend shared with me how he loved Katie's spunk and that she was "bold, assertive and told it how it was." He said the best part of her spunk, though, was her smile because after she spoke her mind, she gave you a smile so full of love you didn't even mind. Another friend called it her "secret sass." She spoke of Katie's laugh and how it seemed to explode out of her, unable to be contained.

Katie loved playing a game called "Grandma's Underpants" with a few friends. The object of the game was to answer any and every question with the words, "Grandma's underpants" WITHOUT laughing. Katie's giggles inevitably slipped out, making it difficult for her to ever win.

She could also do the very best eye roll, so Chad and I celebrated that for her. We would say, "Oh that was really good. Do it again!" Sometimes she laughed then, and, well, sometimes she didn't.

I enjoyed Katie's humor so very much. She liked puns and corny jokes the best of all. This was one of her favorite witticisms:

> A linguistics professor was lecturing to his class one day. "In English," he said, "a double negative forms a positive. In some languages though, such as Russian, a double negative is still a negative. However," he pointed out, "there is no language wherein a double positive can form a negative."
>
> A voice from the back of the room piped up, "Yeah, right."

◁

Katie

Faith

I chose this word for 2017 because it is something I've pushed away for a while. It's always been there but my faith has been pushed into the background for far too long now. In 2017, I really want to bring my faith into the foreground. This year, my God time will become daily and I will really develop my life around my faith. It will become what it should have become years ago, my true rock and foundation for my life.

I will find a time to spend time in the Word and talking to God, as well as just making time to listen daily. I'll never truly hear God if I don't make time to just listen for him. I need to make time to just rest and rejoice in His amazing creation. I want to slow down my life and look around. I want to thank Him and praise Him for how blessed I am.

In the past, I have only spent time with God if I felt like it and to be honest, that wasn't very often. Maybe twice a week on a good week, which is absolutely not enough. I think and hope to see a difference in my attitude towards life and others. I hope to just overall mend my relationship with God. It's like a bridge with some pieces missing and, in 2017, I want to put all of the pieces back in place.

There were many other words that I could have chosen, but I felt that this word encompassed all of them. Wisdom, joy, patience, and love, to name a few. Growing my faith will bring me more of all of these.

I'm going to fight back with joy. I will make laughter, smiling, dancing, and singing a normal thing to do. I'm going to appreciate the joy bombs that life brings. I don't want them to go unnoticed and unappreciated any longer. In the past, I've thought that joy and happiness were the same thing. However, recently I've realized they are definitely not. I cannot be happy and sad at the same time, but I can be joyful and sad at the same time. Regardless of my circumstances or how I feel, I can choose to act and respond in joy.

As I read through the Bible, I want to not just read but devour the words on the page. As I sing on Sunday mornings, I want to not just sing the words on the screen but worship God through song. As I go through life, I want to not just go through life but go through life spreading God's love and joy for us.

2017 will be my year to remember. In the future when I give my testimony, I want to be able to say that this was the year my faith grew stronger than ever before. This is not a New Year's Resolution. This is a New Life Resolution. And it all starts now!

Sarah

When Katie chose *Faith* as her resolution word for 2017, she was right in the middle of her first six months of cancer treatment. I am amazed at her desire for spiritual growth in the midst of this trial in her life. She wrote that her faith had been in the background of her life and she wanted to bring it to the foreground. Now, I don't pretend to know everything that was going on in my teenage daughter's head or her life, but I have read enough of her journals to support my belief that she was already living a life that pointed to God. Yet her relationship with him continued to mature.

Faith, joy, peace and love are not attributes some people have and others do not. They are fruits that develop and sweeten when we are firmly attached to the vine… the branch… the trunk… the roots of God. Even as Katie wrote these words for her eighth-grade English class, she was making a choice to pursue God and to seek out opportunities to be joyful, to worship and to encourage. Her writings remind me that even though life was not going the way she had hoped, she made a conscious decision to stay connected to God.

I love that Katie says 2017 would be her year to remember because after returning home from her extended hospitalization in Cincinnati, she had an extraordinary few months. She was so sick on the inside but somehow her body and spirit just kept enjoying life. Before we even left Cincinnati, she went to Kings Island with her large extended family—grandparents, aunts, uncles, cousins. She did not have the physical ability to walk around an amusement park all day, so she casually rode along in a double stroller beside a younger cousin, getting up for brief rides on the mini-roller coasters and carousels.

She spent long days at the pool with her friends, sporting a baseball cap over her bald head. She walked with Ben, Annie and Daniel to the nearby convenience store to buy slushies and then to the little league field to play on the playground. She wandered the neighborhood with her friend, Naomi, discussing plans for high school in the fall. She sat on Thessa's back porch where they taught her dog new tricks while plotting out their futures. She played with puppies and sorted books with Helen, a teacher and family friend. These were the activities Katie loved— simply being present, laughing, smiling, and appreciating the people in her life.

On Sundays, Katie planned a picnic at church with her friend, Alyssa. After they attended the worship service and while they waited for both sets of parents to finish other obligations, they sat in a quiet office, eating Velveeta shells and cheese while they talked and laughed about everything. Sometimes, she and Alyssa walked across the street to Taco Bell for their picnic. Katie, who did not eat any type of Mexican cuisine, loved Taco Bell only for their frozen drinks which left her mouth a bright bluish-green color. Afterward, as they sat together in the office or in Alyssa's car, they videoed themselves singing to music with Katie's blue tongue flashing on every word. She captioned one of their Instagram pics, "if you don't go to taco bell and eat velveeta on sundays, then you're not churching right!"

I accompanied Katie on a couple short trips with friends that summer. I took her and two friends, Kenzie and Faith, to a cabin in Pocahontas County, West Virginia for a few days. The girls had no plans other than to enjoy the time away together, sitting outside on the porch in the sunshine. On another occasion, when Katie had appointments in Cincinnati that spanned three days, she invited Thessa and Alyssa to join us. During that trip, we shopped most of the time Katie was not at the hospital, ate at Olive Garden more than once, and smeared on face masks while watching movies at the hotel. One night while there, we all sat up bleary-eyed as Katie yelled in her sleep, "No! No!" Then we laughed immensely when she explained that, in her dream, she was trying to protect her chicken nuggets from the hands of her much bigger friends, Rodger and Robert. Such fun memories from those little adventures.

Katie loved having her nails manicured, occasionally adding acrylic nails and fun gel colors. It was not a normal part of our budget but rather a pleasure gifted to her by several people during her illness. She eagerly accepted each invitation for a manicure or a pedicure with her grandma or one of her four aunts, carefully planning them just far enough apart to keep her nails lovely. These little pockets of pampered time were such a gift to her after months in a hospital. One day in July, Katie, Annie, and I decided to use a gift certificate and plan a girls' spa day, but some difficult circumstances interrupted my ability to join them. Providentially, my sister-in-law happened to be visiting that week and was able to spend the day with Katie and Annie in my place. While I am sorry I had to miss that time with my girls, I am grateful they had the opportunity to make another sweet memory together with family.

Perhaps the best part of the summer was the week we spent in Florida. Soon after her discharge from the hospital in June, Dr. Robin suggested we plan a vacation. More than anyone, she knew the trauma we had experienced over the previous few months and how desperately we wanted to enjoy time with all five of our kids together. She also knew best the tenacity of Katie's disease and the value of every day we could embrace. So, when she said go, we made it happen. Katie had always wanted to visit a beach with white sand and clear blue water, so we called in a quick favor from our friends who own a house on the Gulf coast of Florida. I recall that trip with such affection because Katie was at her physical best that week. She laid by the ocean and kayaked in the nearby lake. She ate popsicles and drove go-karts. She floated in the pool and took silly pictures with Daniel. It would be misleading to tell you that my kids loved every moment of being together that week because they didn't. Within an hour of our arrival, they were arguing over who would sleep in what room, all choosing the exact same bed out of the seven available. The kids who wanted to stay by the ocean fussed at the ones who wanted to sit by the television. Some wanted fast food for dinner while others wanted a nice slow meal. We even played a round of miniature golf for Daniel, knowing that it would turn into one big fracas like always. Regardless, we still had a lot of fun that week. And we were still all together. And it was one of the ways 2017 became a year to remember- not just for Katie, but for all of us.

◁

Katie

Rest in God's presence, allowing Him to take charge of the day.

Don't bolt like a racehorse suddenly released.

Walk purposefully with God, allowing Him to direct my course one step at a time.

Thank God for each blessing along the way—this brings joy to both me and God.

A grateful ♡ protects me from negative thinking.

Thankfulness allows me to see the abundance He showers on me daily.

In everything give thanks, for this is God's will for me.

Colossians 4:2

1 Thessalonians 5:18

Devote yourselves to prayer, being watchful and thankful.

— Colossians 4:2

… give thanks in all circumstances; for this is God's will for you in Christ Jesus.

— 1 Thessalonians 5:18

Sarah

In our small town, there is a favorite barber shop called Rick's Place. Rick has cut the hair of half the men in town and holds the respect of everyone. After I failed in an attempt to trim the thick locks and double crown of my oldest son when he was a toddler, I decided we were just going to get to know this man named Rick. So every few weeks, I took my kids and waited for our turn at the barber shop, sitting amid men and boys, walls plastered with old license plates, an overflowing magazine rack, a loud TV in the corner, and a bathroom that was a bit questionable for my girls. Our entrance became more and more grand as we had more and more kids. I stood there, bouncing a baby on my hip, trying to pacify a toddler and attempting to entertain a preschooler, while conversations about dogs and motorcycles and fishing carried on around me.

Investing our money and time and a little bit of our lives into Rick's Place proved to be one of the best decisions. For more than 15 years, one Cobb boy after another has sat in his chair. And every time we turn to leave, with a true heart of gratitude, Rick says "Hey guys... thanks for coming in." Could it be that God directs our steps even to the point of the barber we frequent? I think, perhaps, yes.

In August 2017, I was at Rick's with the boys getting back-to-school haircuts while Chad and Katie were in Cincinnati. This was supposed to be a quick day trip for Katie's immunotherapy infusion which should have had them back on the road in just a couple hours. Instead, she had mentioned her recent headaches to her oncologist which led to a CT scan and a long wait for results. A short day turned into a long day for all of us. I had already talked with Katie earlier in the day, trying to allay her terror around why they were doing a scan and what this could possibly indicate. I had been expecting a call throughout the afternoon with final CT results and was now a bit frustrated and edgy as I stood in the barber shop having not heard from them.

My phone rang and I stepped out the back door of the shop to talk to Chad. He anxiously reported that the CT scan showed the lymphoma had spread to the dura (the lining) around her brain. What? How could that be? Weren't these headaches simply related to a slight cold she had been fighting? I understood the words, but I was still having trouble comprehending the implications. The oncologist got on the phone to speak with me as I eased myself to my knees on the little back deck of the barber shop. MRI early next week. Proton radiation to begin the following week. Lung and brain radiation being planned now. Even after I hung up the phone, I stayed in that position for several minutes, putting my head down into my hands as the thought of all this made me weak. More bad news. Exponentially worse than bad news. Why always bad news, God?

Eventually, I recovered enough to walk back into the shop where Rick had finished with all three boys' hair. I was not ready to talk about this, but my distraught face conveyed more than enough. "I just need you to pray for us," I said with my head hanging low and tears in my eyes. Rick hugged me and refused to allow me to pay that day, saying, "Your money is no good here." Rick's Place is more than just a haircut. More like a blessing along the way.

◁

Katie

Well, hello beautiful! I hope your day has been wonderful and if it hasn't, I hope this post will brighten it up. This week, I am talking about self-image. This is something I struggle with a lot. I'm always worried about what the world thinks of me. Do I look fat? Will they approve of my outfit? Why don't I have abs yet? Is my makeup okay? I'm always comparing myself to others. There is always someone that I am jealous of. Today's generation only wants to focus on the outward appearance, but what matters is on the inside. God doesn't care if you have hair, if you have eyelashes, if you have eyebrows, if you wear makeup or not, if you're 70 or 200 pounds. He doesn't care if you play sports, if you wear sweats or dresses, or if you have straight teeth or not. He just doesn't look at that, what He looks at is your heart. Romans 12:1-2 talks about not conforming to this world. Don't let what everyone else thinks change who you are, God is the only judge.

The first set of verses I have is Ephesians 1:4-5, "God chose us to belong to Christ before the world was even created. He chose us to be holy and without blame in His eyes. He loved us... He adopted us as His children with all the rights children have. He did it because of what Jesus Christ has done." Did you just see that? God chose you! He adopted you and loves no matter what. He didn't adopt you because of what you look like or what sports you play or your size. God adopted you because of His amazing love for you. He doesn't listen to the world's comments, doesn't care what everyone thinks, He loves you. He always has and always will, your Father in heaven will never leave your side. Give God your cup of worries and let Him guzzle it down!

This next verse just goes right along with that. Psalm 139:14. You were fearfully and wonderfully made. We praise God for that. Your works are amazing! You have to learn to accept that this is you, this is who you are. Before you love others, you have to learn to love yourself. Don't ever doubt for one second that you aren't beautiful because you are! God loves you more than you could ever imagine. You are amazing and wonderful and without doubt, you are the best you there can be. That is something worthy of praise!

My last verse that I have for you is from Genesis 1:27. It says, "God created us in His own image. He created us in His own likeness." Can you believe that? The God who created every single thing thought about you and chose exactly how you were to be. Psalm 139:13 says we were completely and fully loved before we were in our mother's womb. Your Father in heaven knows every single hair on your head! Sometimes we think that God doesn't have time for us but a God that knows exactly how many hairs you have is always thinking about you. You really are never alone. Lean on Him in times of doubt and struggle, let Him be your strength and your shield. When the world takes shots at your self-confidence, hold tight to the One that loves you.

Each of these verses just hit home for me. I really felt called to share this with you because if you are struggling with this, then we can fight it together! I feel that God's purpose for me is to be a shoulder for the hurting to cry on, to be a friend for the joyful to laugh with, and to be a disciple for the one and only Father of Creation. Even if you don't struggle with self-image, I'm sure you know someone that does. I encourage you to share this with that person. If you can help, then help! This week, I want to encourage you to listen to the song, "Just As I Am."

I'm usually not one to listen to traditional hymns, but this song's words are so incredible. It says that God accepts you just as you are! Is that not just so wonderful? We are a broken people, we are completely imperfect, but God accepts you just like that. Nothing makes a person more beautiful than the belief that they are beautiful. I really hope that you got something out of this post to apply to your day to day life.

Sarah

As Katie went back to school in the spring, deep under the cover of her cute hats, her hair had just begun to grow again. When her cancer brutally returned in April and another course of harsh chemotherapy was begun, she complained of pain on her scalp. After allowing me to check for any sores or areas of irritation, she said solemnly, "Oh, I know. It's probably my hair falling out again." Sure enough. A couple days later, those tiny little hairs were filling up the inside of her beanie again.

By the time Katie was released from her extended hospitalization and was preparing to start high school in the fall, she actually had short brown hairs tightly pressed all over her head. She was almost ready to move ahead without a hat. While she was trying out looks in her room one day, she sent me a selfie wearing an adorable headband and no hat. She said, "I think I can do this." Her new hair was the color of my natural hair. We used to joke that her hair may come in different, perhaps like mine, and she would say, "You mean, gray?" Touché, Katie, touché. But no, actually, I meant dark brown and wavy.

Katie was told by the oncologist that she would undoubtedly lose her hair again when she began the proton radiation therapy. Again? Ugh. Another devastating blow. It was just now starting to really grow, and it was soft and full and about an inch in length. How many times did she have to deal with this? Wasn't the double dose of radiation enough? This just felt like too much to bear. Less than three weeks after that hatless selfie, as we were driving to Cincinnati for another week of therapy, she informed me that her hair was starting to fall out again. When she woke up the next morning, she said, "Yep, it's all gone." At least it was fast this time. Really, what other positive was there?

The weekend prior, we had celebrated Annie's September birthday with a pool party. Katie felt terrific that day and, for the first time in ten months, she took off her hat as she laughed and swam and did backflips off the diving board without any limitation. How I wish I had a picture or video of that! But I don't. That day, I just sat in the moment, experiencing all of who Katie was. A girl of determination, strength and beauty—beauty that was much deeper than her skin or her hair. A girl made beautiful because she believed that God created her that way.

Well, hello beautiful, you are radiating Jesus.

Katie

Strive to trust God in all areas of your life.

You can grow from the things that make you anxious.

There are blessings hidden in the difficulties.

Don't waste energy regretting the way things are or how they could've been.

Start @ the present moment.

ACCEPT it EXACTLY as it is.

Search for God's way in the midst of those circumstances.

Trust is like a staff you can lean on as you journey uphill with God.

If you trust in Him consistently, the staff will bear as much of your weight as needed.

Psalm 52:8

Proverbs 3:5-6

But I am like an olive tree flourishing in the house of God; I trust in God's unfailing love for ever and ever.
— Psalm 52:8

Trust in the Lord with all your heart and lean not on your own understanding; in all your ways submit to him, and he will make your paths straight.
— Proverbs 3:5-6

Sarah

For months while Chad and I were staying in Cincinnati, we received reports from my family members who were staying with our kids that Annie was routinely having welts appear on her arms and legs. She had always been prone to attracting more mosquito bites than the other kids and I knew they were likely running around outside late into the evenings, so I continued to remind her to apply bug-spray. My family was concerned about hives stemming from anxiety with the situation, but they looked like insect bites, so I pushed the insect repellent. Plus, it was such a minor complaint compared to what I was dealing with in Katie's hospital room every day and, honestly, I could only handle so much. So, I mostly disregarded Annie's small, red, itchy bumps and, thankfully, they seemed to subside a little after we came home from Cincinnati, too.

Until… one night… when I saw a bug slipping under Annie's pillowcase as I was tucking her into bed. I grabbed that skinny little red critter between my fingers and held it there inconspicuously as I kissed her forehead and pleasantly told her good night. As I hurried downstairs to place it in a sandwich bag and search its appearance on the internet, I instantly realized what it must be.

Bed bugs.

First thing the next morning, I began a search. I started stripping beds and washing sheets. At first, I only found two bugs on Annie's entire bed and none elsewhere in the house. Whew. *We must have caught them early*, I thought. This would not be so difficult after all. Because I didn't really have time for this, ya know. Not that any of us have time planned into our lives for mediocre crises, but Katie was in the middle of receiving proton radiation in Cincinnati Monday through Friday every week. The next day, I would be packing up to leave again with her and Daniel for several days. There was no way I had time to remove and heat dry every piece of fabric in my house, sort through every item in every bedroom, or deal with the logistics and expense of an exterminator. So, this was very good that there were only a few lone bugs.

But as I sat in my kitchen that Saturday afternoon, listening to my dryer rotate many loads of clothes, I remembered… Annie had not been sleeping in her bed. During the time we were in Cincinnati… during the time she had those itchy bites appear every single day, she was sleeping in the bed Chad and I share.

She could not bear to sleep in her room alone—without Katie's presence—so she always slept in our room with whomever was staying there with my kids. My room. My bed. No. No, that couldn't possibly be it. Could it? I had already washed and dried the sheets. That should have been enough, right? No. I didn't even want to check. I didn't really want to know.

I walked into my bedroom and pushed the mattress off the side, revealing the top of the box springs underneath. As I did, the bugs began to scurry away from the light I had exposed them to, and I started grabbing them between my fingers. I am not exaggerating at all. I yelled for Ben to bring me a sandwich bag so I could contain them. Then I hoisted the box springs up on its end and leaned it against the headboard. And there they were. Hundreds and hundreds of them. Lining the underside of my bed, crowded together on the bottom of the box springs and along the side rails.

I fell onto my knees in my bedroom floor, in the middle of my torn-apart bed, and cried. With my head on the floor, I just laid there and sobbed. And then I yelled, "Really, God? Really?! Bed bugs? You have gotta be freaking kidding me!!!!"

Daniel and Ben came around the corner to see what was wrong. As they saw me, Ben very graciously turned Daniel around, taking him out of the room, saying, "Come on, let's leave Mommy alone."

I called my sister Mary who pretty much took care of everything for me. She came and vacuumed all of those bugs, stifling her gags when she saw the hordes of them under the nightstands and in the corners by the bed. Our bedroom and the girls' bedroom were stripped down to furniture only. Every drawer, every article of clothing, every knick-knack, every book, every shoe, every paper was removed and placed into a tote or a trash bag. The closets and storage eaves were emptied of all clothes, hand me down items, luggage and Christmas decorations. For the next week, while I was out of town with Katie, Chad, my mom, and my sisters took everything—and I mean everything—to the laundromat to be dried on high heat for an extended cycle. If it wasn't able to go into the dryer, it was sprayed with alcohol. Then I drove back from Cincinnati only to spend the day away from home while the exterminator sprayed throughout the house multiple times.

For several weeks we lived out of totes of clothes in our garage. Before taking a shower in the morning or evening, we walked to the garage to select our outfits and underwear and shoes for the day. Every decoration, book, and random item was in a bag or box there as well. Our house and life were in disarray. Looking back, I am not sure how I even managed that season. It was as if I had nothing left of my own strength and all my weight was leaning on God. I had to ACCEPT it EXACTLY as it was.

But I still don't understand... why the bed bugs? In the midst of that nightmare, God... why the bed bugs?

◁

Katie

Deuteronomy 6:4-9

I am a huge influence in the lives of those around me. Don't drop the responsibility onto someone else because you think they might be a little better at teaching/influencing.

Take responsibility. Do your job.

My time is limited. Psalm 90:12

Imagine the END. What really matters??

The ultimate goal: who do I want them to become? Luke 2:52

Celebrate the milestones. Fight for the HEART ♡

Invest in the relationship. Influence is EARNED.

Spend quality, unstructured time.

Leave no doubt that they are loved. Luke 3:22

Hear, O Israel: The Lord our God, the Lord is one. Love the Lord your God with all your heart and with all your soul and with all your strength. These commandments that I give you today are to be on your hearts. Impress them on your children. Talk about them when you sit at home and when you walk along the road, when you lie down and when you get up. Tie them as symbols on your hands and bind them on your foreheads. Write them on the doorframes of your houses and on your gates.

— Deuteronomy 6:4-9

Teach us to realize how short our lives are. Then our hearts will become wise.

— Psalm 90:12 (NIrV)

Jesus became wiser and stronger. He also became more and more pleasing to God and to people.

— Luke 2:52 (NirV)

The Holy Spirit came to rest on him in the form of a dove. A voice came from heaven. It said, "You are my Son, and I love you. I am very pleased with you."

— Luke 3:22 (NIrV)

Sarah

The Suite Life of Daniel and Katie. That's what Katie called it.

During the time she was receiving proton radiation therapy, we lived in a hotel suite in Cincinnati Monday through Friday. Katie had appointments every day at the Liberty campus of the hospital on the north side of Cincinnati and a couple days each week at the main campus on the south side of Cincinnati, so we found a place to stay somewhere in between. Chad stayed at home with the other kids most of the week as he worked and they attended school; he then swapped places with me on Thursday morning so that I could be at home with the kids and he could be present with Katie. Because Daniel wasn't in school yet, it was logistically easier for him to go to Cincinnati with Katie and me to enjoy the *suite life.* Katie dubbed it such because she had grown up watching *The Suite Life of Zack and Cody* on The Disney Channel and, well, sometimes life is what you make of it. And she was rather adept at making it seem better than it really was.

Most of Katie's radiation appointments were in the morning so we headed to the hospital after enjoying the hotel breakfast. The child life therapist at the Liberty oncology department made a small box for Daniel with his name on it. In it she placed some dinosaurs and superheroes and, occasionally, another small surprise, before she tucked it behind the desk where we checked in each day. It was something special for him to have while we waited for Katie to finish her treatment.

The treatments were difficult for Katie. Proton therapy is a very precise type of radiation treatment where the exact tissue is targeted and destroyed by the beam of protons. In order for that to be effective and to reduce any unintended effects on other tissue, Katie had to lie incredibly still on a flat table that rose into the air while the massive equipment in the room circled around her for close to an hour. *Flat* is kind of an understatement as she described it more like a slab of concrete. Not only were her arms and chest strapped onto the table to prohibit movement of her torso but, during the time she was receiving therapy to the lining around her brain, she also had to wear a breathable mask that firmly fastened her head in one position. After situating her, the technicians left the treatment room to stand behind a barrier while they executed the radiation. Imagine the anxiety surrounding that set up. Of course, they tried their very best to support her through various means. One thing that helped tremendously was the use of her own music. Katie put together a playlist on Spotify for her time in radiation, and the technicians played it over the speaker into the room for her to hear. The playlist revealed her eclectic taste in music as a country song followed a pop song that followed a contemporary Christian song.

After the radiation treatment finished for the day—and if there were no other appointments scheduled—we had the rest of the day to ourselves. Sometimes we went shopping or to a park or to the pool at the hotel suite. We took our game system and Katie taught Daniel how to play Mario Kart. We visited the zoo and saw Fiona, the baby hippopotamus. We found The Cone, an iconic little Cincinnati ice cream vendor with all sorts of fun and yumminess. Eventually, we made our way back to the hotel where Katie did schoolwork while Daniel watched TV and I cooked dinner in the little kitchen. At bedtime, we laid in the king size bed together watching *America's Got Talent*, or another of her favorite shows, before reading a book and drifting off to sleep.

Katie adored Daniel, and she left no doubt that he was loved. She was a huge influence in his four-year-old life, and he loved her so much. It was both a good distraction and a sweet gift that Daniel lived *the suite life* with us for those weeks. It was some of the most quality, unstructured time. They were this fun little duo as she played games and made faces and gave him piggy-back rides. Each night, as I watched them cuddle up together in the bed at the hotel—Daniel always without a shirt, Katie always with a hat—I prayed and begged God to let Daniel remember. Let him remember so much from these years that most kids forget. Let him remember this. Let him remember her.

◁

Katie

The following is a portion of an assignment in which Katie was required to choose a song that revealed a component of her identity.

I chose a song that I could relate to, "King of My Heart," by Kutless. Repeatedly throughout the song, it sings, "You are good..." Daily, I can see this proven in my life. God shows His goodness in so many ways. I am able to be home with my family and friends. I can enjoy the rest of my summer and have a tinge of normalcy back in my routine. He is so good to me because I have proof of physical, emotional and spiritual healing and strengthening in my life. I have been blessed with what feels like some of the best doctors, medical staff, research and medicine. I am immensely grateful for the technology and science we have today. God has shown His goodness through allowing my family to have a vacation and escape the medical world for a week. We can relax, knowing He will continue to provide goodness and mercy and healing upon us. The song also states, "You're never gonna let, never gonna let me down..." In the past ten months, my life has been in a bit of a crazy situation. I have gone through so much more than anyone should ever have to go through. I have been on the verge of life and death at times, but the King of my heart has never let me down. He is not done with me yet, the Author is still perfecting His story. I have faith and trust in Him and His grip on my life that I can get through this. The song expresses a part of my identity that is being written right now.

Sarah

Having missed most of her eighth-grade year, Katie was really looking forward to high school with her friends. In August, as we discussed various plans for her treatments, Katie's physicians worked around her strong desire to begin her freshman year at the same time as her peers. The plan was for her to attend school for about three weeks and become comfortable in her classes before returning to Cincinnati for the proton radiation therapy. Unfortunately, when the lymphoma was found to have spread to the outside of her brain, the urgency for radiation trumped the previous plan.

After four days of high school, Katie switched to homebound instruction. For a child who loves the socialization and the academics of school, this was yet another sucker punch. Unfair. Vicious. Painful.

While Katie was shuffled back and forth to Cincinnati, other students made preparations for Winfield High School Homecoming. Homecoming is an important event in high school with the selection of an attendant from each class and the crowning of the homecoming queen during halftime of the football game. There is also a pep rally, tailgating and a parade before the game. And, of course, the homecoming dance. Definitely an opportunity for the school and entire community to come together.

During this time of planning, Katie's classmates chose her to be the homecoming attendant for the freshman class. She was so surprised and over-the-moon excited when she received the news! All smiles and blushed cheeks, she kept asking, "Are you serious?!?" She felt incredibly honored and loved by this gesture, and she hesitated very little before asking her friend, Joey, to be her escort for the event. Joey and Katie had been friends since kindergarten, and he was thrilled to stand beside her as he cared so much for her.

When the decision was made to expedite the proton radiation treatments, we also elected to work with Make-A-Wish to plan Katie's trip to Hawaii as soon as possible. We wanted her to be at her best for the trip, so it was scheduled for the week following her final proton therapy treatment. The timing was perfect because she would return from Hawaii (*with a tan*, she reminded me) and be able to attend school the day of homecoming and to participate in all of the festivities with her friends.

We did not have much time for the usual homecoming preparations. Between finishing therapy in Cincinnati and packing for Hawaii (remember, all our clothes were still in totes in the garage during this time), we also needed to find her a dress and accessories and a car to ride in during the parade. Given more time, I expect we would have searched high and low for the right dress. But our time was limited to one afternoon following her appointment to check labs and receive a blood transfusion. Although it was sometimes difficult for Katie to find stylish and age-appropriate fashions for her incredibly small stature, within a couple hours of searching we found a lace-covered maroon dress with long sleeves that perfectly matched her favorite hat. Joey would wear a black suit with a maroon vest as his six feet of young manliness towered over her four and a half feet of fragile beauty.

However, the following week, while we were in Hawaii, Katie's health began to deteriorate quickly. When we made the difficult decision to return home early, Katie was fully aware that she would not be able to attend the homecoming game. After all the quick but elating preparation, she knew she would not be able to participate like she had planned. Like she had hoped. She presumed that, once again, she would be in Cincinnati, watching all the excitement unfold on Instagram while Joey stood alone in her place. It was yet another unexpected hit. One more experience that cancer stole from her. This was not the way it was supposed to be.

I sure do feel like you left us alone, God. Is this really part of Katie's story? Is this how you supposedly perfect it? Can I even trust you anymore?

◁

Katie

Hope is oxygen to the believer who is short of breath.

Hope is the life preserver we cling to when everything says let go.

Place your hope in him!

Romans 12:12

Romans 5:1-5

Jesus came hope-filled to make us hopeful.

Trouble produces patience. Patience produces character. Character produces hope. Hope produces another reason to REJOICE.

Even in the toughest of times, God is doing something in and through us.

♡ filled with heavenly hope!

1 Corinthians 15:42-44

RENEW YOUR HOPE IN HIM

ANCHOR IN HIS JOY

Be joyful in hope, patient in affliction, faithful in prayer.

— Romans 12:12

Therefore, since we have been justified through faith, we have peace with God through our Lord Jesus Christ, through whom we have gained access by faith into this grace in which we now stand. And we boast in the hope of the glory of God. Not only so, but we also glory in our sufferings, because we know that suffering produces perseverance; perseverance, character; and character, hope. And hope does not put us to shame, because God's love has been poured out into our hearts through the Holy Spirit, who has been given to us.

— Romans 5:1-5

It will be like that with bodies that are raised from the dead. The body that is planted does not last forever. The body that is raised from the dead lasts forever. It is planted without honor. But it is raised in glory. It is planted in weakness. But it is raised in power. It is planted as an earthly body. But it is raised as a spiritual body.

— 1 Corinthians 15:42-44 (NIrV)

Sarah

Hawaii brought hope.

Make-A-Wish is an incredible organization that brings hope and happiness to kids and families when they need it most. All through her illness, Katie had hoped to go to Hawaii through the support of Make-A-Wish. That's a pretty significant request—especially with the size of our family—but Katie was dreaming big and refused to ask for anything less. After we received word that the Hawaii trip might really happen, Katie wanted to wait to travel until after her treatments were finished and her strength and hair were returning so that she could enjoy it to the utmost. However, when the scans started looking worse in the fall of 2017 and after her primary and radiation oncologists gave their blessings, we asked Make-A-Wish to plan the trip for as soon as possible. Make-A-Wish organized that trip in less than two weeks with complete arrangements for everything we needed.

We left for Hawaii early on October 3rd, traveling for about 16 hours across three flights, arriving in Honolulu late in the evening. Katie began feeling a little short of breath as we traveled, making our way through multiple airports during the day, and she was completely exhausted by the time we arrived at our suite at the Sheraton Waikiki. As I tucked her into bed, she felt hot against my hands. Surely this was not a fever. Surely. I was immediately furious and petrified. In my angst, I struggled to find the thermometer in my luggage as I phoned the on-call oncologist at Cincinnati Children's Hospital. "Go to the emergency room," was the immediate answer. I begged them to give me their favor to not take her. "I'll give her Tylenol and begin the steroids we brought just in case," I pleaded. "Please, we just got here, and we are all exhausted." But when I found the thermometer, Katie's temperature had already risen to 104 degrees. I had no choice in this matter.

Around 11 p.m., we left the kids in bed with Aaron at the hotel while Chad drove Katie and me to the nearby hospital only two miles away. By God's grace, it was the only hospital in Hawaii with a pediatric oncology department. She was assessed, X-rayed, and given antibiotics. She was very stable at that time, and I again begged and pleaded them to not admit her overnight. I promised to bring her back immediately if she worsened. The emergency room physician, although reluctant, agreed to let us return to the hotel and follow up the next day with the outpatient oncology clinic.

I spoke with Katie's physician from Cincinnati on the phone several times, despite the six-hour time difference between us. She and the radiation oncologist reviewed the X-rays and labs from the emergency room. They were lovingly honest with me. Dr. Robin said:

> This is most likely the cancer progressing. Not inflammation from the radiation or another infection. The lymphoma appears to have broken through the treatments that were keeping it in check. We know her cancer progresses quickly and there is no guarantee how much time that will take. I know she wanted this trip and we want her to enjoy it as much as she can, but you need to realize that if she worsens quickly, you may get stuck there. You will have to decide.

There was so much to comprehend in those few words and so much weight in the outcome. And by the next day, we made the very difficult decision to shorten our trip.

The local chapter of Make-A-Wish worked quickly to change our itinerary so we could still enjoy as much of Hawaii as possible in the few days we were there. We traveled up the beautiful coastline of Oahu, stopping at several vantage points as we made our way to the Polynesian Cultural Center for a luau dinner and show. We splashed in the pool and slipped down the waterslides at the Sheraton. We buried our toes in the sand on Waikiki Beach. We walked down the shoreline for dinner, tasted malasada doughnuts, and devoured Hawaiian shaved ice for at least one meal every day.

During that time, Katie had intermittent fevers and pain in her back and pelvic bones. She became short of breath with any exertion and sometimes even at rest. Katie's spirited determination normally led her to hate using a wheelchair, but she did not refuse any help that week. By employing a wheelchair during excursions and either Chad or Aaron giving her piggyback rides, we did not allow her to walk more than about 50 feet at any one time.

Part of Katie's wish for Hawaii was to swim with dolphins at Sea Life Park and Make-A-Wish had arranged that for us. Knowing Katie would not participate if she had to swim with her head uncovered and having learned no loose items were allowed in the pool with the dolphins, I bought a swim cap with a chin strap for her to wear. Katie said it looked like something from the 1950s, and she was less than thrilled about wearing it, but she was willing to do so in order to have that experience. When it was time to get dressed for the swim, Katie first went into the changing room alone and then called to me to help with the swim cap. I walked into the stall, shutting the door behind me, as she bowed her head in front of me and removed her baseball cap. Sigh. I never got used to seeing that bald representation of everything broken in her life. I quickly situated the ugly white swim cap on her head, and we made our way out to the pool. As I gathered her lifejacket and pushed her wheelchair to the appropriate area, I thought, *I must be crazy. I am getting ready to put my daughter—who can hardly walk without becoming short of breath— into a pool to swim with dolphins. This is ridiculous.* But then I corrected myself, *No, this is exactly what she wanted to do. I am not taking it away from her. And Satan can go to hell before I let him take it either.* Truly, watching Katie swim with the dolphins that day is one of my most precious memories of her determination.

Snorkeling was the other activity that Katie was really looking forward to in Hawaii. We woke up early on our very last day so that we could drive to Hanauma Bay first thing. All of us really wanted to have this opportunity even though a little extra sleep sounded much more appealing at that point. Once again, Katie and I walked into the changing room on the beach and she bowed her bald head in front of me so that I could place her swim cap. That humble position exemplified the depth of her desire to live every moment to its fullest.

It was around 8 a.m. when we made our way out to the chilly water with masks and snorkels and flippers in tow. Chad and the others ran on ahead, not allowing the cool temperature to dampen their excitement, while Katie eased into the water, one small step at a time. She tried and tried for a long time, but she could never adjust to the water's cold temperature. I knew she longed to try snorkeling and see the array of fish in the reef so I encouraged her to put her head under even for a minute, but she just could not. The cold took her breath and it was simply more than she could cope with at that point. She finally smiled slightly and said, "I'll just go sit on the sand. I mean, sitting on the beach in Hawaii isn't really that bad." After a few minutes, Annie made her way to the towel beside Katie and they sat there together for a long time. Chad and Ben were snorkeling alongside one another. Aaron swam with Daniel on his back, indicating to Daniel when to lean his head into the water to see the colorful fish. I stood in the shallow water, shifting my focus between these scenes. With tears in my eyes, I said aloud, "God, I love these kids."

The evening before we left, Katie expressed to me that even though she was disappointed that the trip had to be shortened, she really just wanted to go home. She had tried her best to smile and enjoy Hawaii while we were there, but by then, she felt so poorly and knew she was not well. She had hoped for that trip for so long, and it made me so sad and mad to watch the fullness of it taken from her. She had endured so much without complaining, and she deserved to have a week of fun and sheer enjoyment, forgetting about the cancer that had robbed her of so much in the past year.

Yes, the week in Hawaii was difficult and challenging and stressful in every way. Yet, by God's grace, it was also beautiful and incredible and fulfilling. Looking back, Hawaii gave more than it took. It gave us a sweet time together with extraordinary memories. And it gave hope. Not hope in a miraculous healing. No, Hawaii brought hope that God could do something even better than that.

◁

Katie

Seek Him and I will find more than ever dreamed possible.

Let God replace worry in my life.

He is like a cloud that showers peace into the pool of my mind.

God blesses, I receive and thank him.

God is my goal or finish line of ALL searching.

When lesser goals capture my attention, God goes to the background.

EXPAND your focus!

Let nothing stop my search for God!

Psalm 27:8

Philippians 4:7

Jeremiah 29:13

LORD, I AM COMING!

My heart says of you, "Seek his face!" Your face, Lord, I will seek.

— Psalm 27:8

And the peace of God, which transcends all understanding, will guard your hearts and your minds in Christ Jesus.

— Philippians 4:7

You will seek me and find me when you seek me with all your heart.

— Jeremiah 29:13

Sarah

We left Hawaii at 10:30 p.m. local time on October 7th and flew through the night, landing at 7 a.m. local time in Los Angeles. Everyone slept through the first leg of our trip except me. Daniel was asleep next to me before we took off and did not awake until we landed. Katie also slept beside me and did not appear to be distressed at all during the flight. That was a direct YES from God. Before we left for the airport, she had been sitting on the couch, breathing quick and shallow breaths, while we hurriedly packed around her. It was the middle of the night at home but I sent out a Mayday call to a few people: Whenever you get this message, you have to pray we can get Katie back safely.

The return trip would have made for a comedic story later if the circumstances had been different. Our first layover was short, and the attendant with the wheelchair for Katie never showed up at our gate, so we grabbed a wheelchair that was sitting empty and began to navigate through a crowded Los Angeles airport. There was no quick breakfast food to be found nearby, so Chips Ahoy and Honey Buns had to work for the seven of us. The next flight took us across the country into Charlotte, North Carolina. About an hour before we landed, Katie had a coughing fit which left her breathing through pursed lips to recover. She and I talked about going to a hospital in Charlotte when we landed there, but she desperately did not want to do that. We only had an hour layover in Charlotte and then a 45-minute flight to West Virginia, so we agreed that if she did not worsen, we could make it those two hours to the hospital in Charleston where at least they knew us. Her breathing settled down and she seemed to be okay for the rest of that flight.

Charlotte was another quick turnaround. The attendant pushing Katie's wheelchair through this airport assisted us in getting some pizzas and drinks on our way from one gate to another. We arrived at the small gate with a few minutes to spare but there were not enough empty seats for all of us to sit together. As I was trying to keep everyone calm and organize us into an area on the floor where we could eat quickly, a gentleman nearby stood up to offer two seats to us, extending grace to our obviously stressed family. Unfortunately, before I could help any of the kids move their food off the floor, another man, paying no attention to anyone other than himself, sat down in the same chair just offered to us and placed his stuff in the chair beside him. *Unbelievable.* Which is what I thought and what the first gentleman said aloud from his new seat. At that point, we simply managed from our current position as best we could. We almost did not even get onto the plane going to Charleston because of a mix-up with the tickets. We were standing at the gate while they closed the boarding lane, begging them to at least let Katie and me onto the plane. Finally, just as they were shutting the flight doors, the attendant who was so adamant about not letting us onto the plane two minutes before, suddenly looked up and said, "Okay, everybody on, just take whatever seats are left, and I will figure out how to enter it into this computer."

During the flight, I told Katie we could go straight to our local hospital once we landed and get a helicopter on its way from Cincinnati immediately. She maintained that she did not want to be transported via helicopter, but then she looked at me and asked, "What do you think?" Such a hard decision. I had been making too many of these hard decisions recently. I wanted to take care of her, but I also wanted to respect her wishes. I asked how she felt about her breathing and told her that we would drive to Cincinnati that night as long as she did not become worse. We had previously hoped to wait until the following morning, but it was becoming obvious that we would not be able to do that. She agreed.

As soon as we landed, we drove the 30 minutes to our home and proceeded to empty all the suitcases onto the living room floor. Chad and I put together a bag for Cincinnati with a couple changes of clothes while Katie sat for a few brief moments in her house… on her steps… petting her dog. She needed that. And I needed that for her. Within the hour, the three of us were back out the door and on our way to Cincinnati while our other kids stayed home with my parents.

We arrived at the emergency room at Cincinnati Children's Hospital around midnight. They were expecting us, as I had been in direct communication with her physicians during these last several days. Upon arrival, her oxygen saturation was in the 70s when it should have been in the 90s. I thought it was simply inaccurate due to her acrylic nails because she did not appear that distressed to me. I mean, we had just driven for three hours and she had not complained whatsoever. Sure, she had sat in the back of the car and had not said much, but she had not seemed to be worsening that quickly either. Yet the reading was accurate, and she was moved immediately to another room for better management of the situation. Within a few minutes after applying the more precise oxygen mask, her oxygen saturation began to recover. Katie was becoming scared, however, and so was I. She had been compensating so hard for so long, and it was almost as if her body began to relax its fight as soon as she got to the place where she felt the safest.

Some hours later, we moved from the emergency room to the PICU and were finally able to close our eyes for a few minutes, completely weary from the circumstances. Early the next morning, while I was lying in bed next to Katie and Chad was dozing in the chair beside us, Dr. Robin walked in. She bent down on the side of the bed near me and I immediately began to cry. "I'm so sorry," I said. "I just didn't know she was that sick." I had been making decisions for days about Katie's care while also trying to give her autonomy in what would become her end-of-life decisions. Dr. Robin touched my arm and gently said, "You gave her a choice. And you got her here. You did the right thing." With a myriad of emotions rising up inside me, those were the words I needed to hear right then.

Katie was snuggled into my chest, so I didn't move when Dr. Robin and Dr. Ben pulled her X-ray up on the monitor. I could see over their shoulders, and it looked so much worse than the one from Honolulu just five days prior. Chad walked out to speak with them while I stayed in bed with her. I didn't need to go. I think I already knew what her physicians were going to report. When Chad returned to the room with tears running down his cheeks, his only words were, "They said… just days." With that, he took his phone and left the room to make a few calls, leaving Katie and me there by ourselves.

Katie was now slightly awake, still snuggled next to me, with her oxygen mask turned up as high as she could tolerate. "What's going on?" she asked. Slowly and gently, I began to speak. "You know how Dr. Norris said she thought your cancer was progressing based on the X-rays taken in Hawaii?" With a deep breath, I went on, "Well, it has progressed even further and there is nothing left that they can do for it."

Katie responded, "Nothing?"

And, with tears in my eyes, I calmly and simply said, "No."

With only the slightest bit of hesitation, she asked, "So… do they think I'm going to die?"

"Yes," I said simply.

"When?" she asked.

I answered her, "Well, no one knows for sure, Katie, but they don't think it will be very long." After a pause, I said, "So Daddy is going to have the other kids come to the hospital."

That was it. That was how I told my 14-year-old daughter she was going to die. It was simple and honest. It was full of emotion but not full of tears. Katie did not scream or cry or beg or question. She simply held my hand. For the next 21 hours, any time I was beside her in bed, she always held my hand.

We made some decisions, along with her physicians, about her plan of care for the next few days. As a nurse, I had some experience with moments like this. Chad, however, had not. And while we were certainly in agreement on how best to care for her, the actual verbalization of those choices was far more harrowing than I had imagined.

From that point forward, Katie used whatever oxygen method she wanted based upon her own comfort level. She received medication for the nausea and dry heaving, and she ate some fruit which gave her a little energy. Continuous morphine began infusing into her IV line which was an excellent medication for managing the coughing fits and the sense of air hunger she felt as the lymphoma took over more and more lung space. She was moved out of the PICU and onto the oncology unit on the 5th floor of the A building. A5. The place where we had lived just a few months prior. The place where the staff had become family. The place where Katie felt safest.

In a way I could barely acknowledge, I had expected Katie's cancer to progress much more slowly. I had anticipated her eventually requiring hospice care and being at home with us during that time. When I realized that was not going to happen, I became angry. In my mind, it was just one more thing cancer had taken from her. Yet God gently, but firmly, showed me nothing was taken. In fact, he had given her a gift. A beautiful gift perfectly suited for Katie.

Because Katie hated awkward. Like most people, she absolutely despised awkward moments and awkward situations, but she was so gracious she rarely said anything to disrupt the interaction or hurt a person's feelings. I tried to manage some of this for her as much as I could, but, in this instance, God managed it. Because of the timeline of events and the location of Cincinnati several hours away from our home, only a few people were able to see Katie that day. Her siblings, her grandparents, her aunts and uncles, her very best friend. And Chevy—the dog she was so fond of—who came to lay on her lap while she rubbed his head. As much as she loved so many people, she would have hated the awkwardness of a parade of people visiting her. For most people in her life, their last interaction was with a smiling, joyful and fun-loving Katie. Which is exactly perfect.

Once our kids arrived, they were in and out of her room several times and, before they left the hospital that evening, they talked about what games we would play together the following day. Because they did not realize that was goodbye, there were no goodbyes. Instead, their parting involved hugs and echoes of, "Love you, Katie," and "See ya in the morning." Daniel walked to her bed to give her their secret handshake. She stuck out her hand and smiled as he gave six squeezes, saying, "1... 2... 3... I... love... you." She grinned as she told him, "You're not supposed to say it." She had always tried to teach him to just squeeze three times to indicate "I love you," but he always said the words instead.

Both Chad and I were able to have some sweet moments with our girl that Monday. I helped her understand a little about the present; Chad helped her understand a little about forever. She was very quiet, but while she said very little, she also never appeared afraid. I could often tell when she was anxious by the way she tapped her nails or fingered her blanket repeatedly, but I do not recall seeing any of those indicators. We cannot predict how we will respond in the face of great distress, but when I remember Katie on that day, the words that come to mind are from 1 John 4:18: "There is no fear in love, but perfect love casts out fear." And as I read the words preceding these, I find: "As we live in God, our love grows more perfect. So we will not be afraid on the day of judgment, but we can face him with confidence because we live like Jesus here in this world." This captures the essence of Katie's story. Katie lived like Jesus here in this world which caused her love to grow. The depth of that love then cast out all fear and enabled her to face her own death with peace and confidence.

After everyone left for the evening, the exhaustion set in for Chad and me as we had only slept somewhere around six hours total over the previous three days. As soon as we turned out the lights, Chad fell asleep sitting in the chair at the bedside, while I snuggled in next to Katie for the first half of the night. She and I were both slipping in and out of sleep, interrupted by her frequent coughing, but resting together, nonetheless. Thanks to the magnificence of morphine, she truly did not appear distressed, despite the waning oxygen capacity of her lungs. Since I had requested all the monitors to be turned off in the room, it was so quiet, with only Katie's iPad playing music as we laid there. She was holding my hand, her beautiful hands and sweet acrylic nails curled around mine. My hands looking so much older next to her soft ones.

At one point, I awoke when I heard her say, "I like those chairs." Realizing she was dreaming, I nudged her and said, "Katie, what kind of chairs are you talking about?" She stirred and laughed a little as she said, "Oh, all this medicine is giving me wacky dreams. They were orange beanbag chairs." I chuckled and said, "Where were they?" She smiled and pointed toward the end of the hospital bed as she said, "Right there." We both smiled as we nestled back to sleep together. A short time after that, Chad and I switched places as he crawled into bed with Katie. I laid down on the pullout chair for a few hours of sleep, thinking we had another long day ahead of us.

Dr. Ben, the attending physician that night, was extra special to us. He always cared for Katie in a very personal way and often came by her room just to sit on her bed for a few minutes and to ask how she was doing. Sometimes he said, "I'm not your doctor today, Katie. I'm just here as your friend." His own children closely parallel the ages of ours, and he often asked about each of our kids by name. Dr. Ben could have gone home that night and spent the evening with his family. After all, he had walked into our room at 8 a.m. that morning and cared for us throughout the day in addition to managing his other patients. He had sat with us that afternoon as we chose comfort for her, and he had shed tears as he reassured us that we had loved her well. Dr. Ben had an oncology fellow and residents who could have remained at the hospital while he slept at home on October 9th. But he chose to stay with us. He was in and out of Katie's room throughout the night, and Dr. Ben was the one who quietly woke me just before 5 a.m. "Sarah, you need to get up."

It was minutes from that point. Minutes of slow soft breaths. Minutes of me lying with my head against hers and Chad burrowed against both our legs. Minutes of *I love you's* spoken again and again in the quiet darkness. Minutes… only minutes… until Dr. Ben gently and lovingly nodded his head to me. Katie's life on earth had ended. She had died. Right there in our arms. Right there where we had laughed about orange beanbag chairs just a few hours prior. And even in those last hours… those last minutes… I enjoyed her. Katie was nothing short of a blessing even then.

As I remember those days, hours and minutes leading up to her death, I recall how God proved to me that nothing was taken. Rather, it was given. The incredible gift of a beautiful death. Without pain. Without fear. Without awkward.

That girl had spent a week in Hawaii—a place she had longed to visit and one of the most beautiful spots on earth. Her body had somehow managed to compensate until she was in the place where she felt the safest, being cared for by Megan, one of the nurses who knew her best. She had spent just a little bit of time with the people she loved the most in this world. She heard her one friend speak for all her friends with the words, "I am going to miss you so much. You are the very best friend." She closed her eyes that night beside her daddy and momma, looking forward to the next day with her family, and she opened her eyes to see Jesus. That was a gift. That was the beautiful grace of God in the midst of a broken world. A truly incredible gift.

◁

Katie

We are short-sighted. Far too easily pleased, far too easily angered. It causes us to be selfish.

Have a deep friendship instead of caring about how many likes you get on a pic.

Instead of being short-sighted, you need to have ETERNAL PERSPECTIVE.

Colossians 3:1-2

Life continues with God!

Since, then, you have been raised with Christ, set your hearts on things above, where Christ is, seated at the right hand of God. Set your minds on things above, not on earthly things.

— Colossians 3:1-2

Sarah

So many times, throughout Katie's struggles, God revealed himself to me very clearly, beginning with the day he told me, "This isn't about you. This is Katie's story." Early in her illness, I felt God put his arm around my shoulder, pull me in tight against him, and say, "I am so, so sorry you have to do this. But, if you will let me, I will go ahead of you and pave this road for you." And there were so many times he did that for us. Often it was through the people he put in our path— the staff, the providers, the people with whom we connected along the way. He walked ahead of us in that the church had recently hired a couple staff members who could conduct some of the teaching and leading while Chad stepped away from those roles for a season. He surrounded us with a family and church and community that loved us well and carried many burdens for us. God answered prayers in ways we did not want. From a perspective we did not have. And with a grace I did not understand at the time.

When we arrived back home on October 10th, 2017, just a few hours after Katie had died, I staggered into my bathroom. Between the whirlwind trip from Hawaii and the days in the hospital, when was the last time I had showered anyhow? Exhausted, I leaned my forehead against the cool wall of the shower and let the hot water rush over me, collecting with the tears as they flowed together down the drain at my feet. In that moment, I felt an abject poverty of spirit. As if I had nothing left to hold in my hands. As if God had taken everything from me. From Katie. And I began to recount to him all the things she had lost. Surely, he needed me to remind him how Katie had missed out on the eighth-grade trip she had raised money for and then watched on Instagram from a hospital room. The homecoming game for which she had been chosen as an attendant but never stood by her escort. The trip to Hawaii which was supposed to be everything she could wish but was interrupted by the menacing laugh of cancer. And what about the graduation she would never walk. The wedding she would never plan. The husband she would never love. The child she would never hold. I listed them for God. All the things that had been taken from her. There were so many. And they kept rolling off my tongue. I could not stop them. I was sad and angry and helpless as I stood there, drenched with water and tears and hurt.

Then God broke into my torrent with his own declaration. Gently, yet firmly, he spoke to me again. "But I restored that today. I restored all of that. Today."

The words stopped. The list stopped. The recitation of hurt stopped. Even the tears seemed to pause temporarily. I could not refute that. Because he had. He had restored all of it that day. Not in the way I would have chosen. Not in the temporal circumstances of homecoming and graduation and a wedding. No, he had restored it through the eternal circumstances of life in heaven. A crown of gold. Length of days forever and ever. The joy of the presence of God. Yes, all the brokenness Katie had and potentially would have experienced in this world had been restored. Given back. Redeemed. In light of eternity, she lost nothing.

It seems as if Katie's journal was written to me... *We are short sighted, Mom. Instead of being short-sighted, you need to have ETERNAL PERSPECTIVE. Life continues with God, don't you remember? I love you, Mom. I'll see you soon.*

◁

Katie

For the highs and lows

and moments between,

mountains and valleys,

and rivers and streams,

For where you are now

and where you will go,

For "I've always known"

and "I told you so,"

For "nothing is happening,"

and "all has gone wrong,"

it is here in this journey

you will learn to be strong

You will get where you're going,

landing where you belong.

-Morgan Harper Nichols

This poem is something I can relate to in my life at this point. It states, "For the highs and lows... for where you are now and where you will go, for 'nothing is happening' and 'all has gone wrong.'" Every day is a new day. I have to take it one moment at a time. One can never know if it will be a day of highs or lows. I have had so many of both in the past few months. Many times, I didn't know what tomorrow would bring or where the day would take me. More than once, I felt hopeless. There was no improvement and some days all we had was news that my health worsened. The poem continues to say, "... it's here in this journey you will learn to be strong..." There is so much truth in that statement. I have become a different person. I am stronger than before. I am a fighter. The piece of poetry finishes by saying, "... you will get where you're going, landing where you belong." What I have gone through is no mistake. I will never understand exactly why this was the path my life went down, but it is a part of my story. When all is through, I will be where God wants me to be in life. There is a greater purpose to this.

Highs and Lows Poem by Morgan Harper Nichols
https://morganharpernichols.com

Sarah

I have enough medical knowledge to understand the final deterioration of Katie's body. I know what was happening to her lungs. The lymphoma rapidly filled every bit of airspace with fluffy tissue and fluid until there was no usable space left for oxygen. Yet I have enough spiritual knowledge to know Katie was already breathing in heaven even as she walked on this earth. The Bible says God "has blessed us in the heavenly realm with every spiritual blessing in Christ" (Ephesians 1:3). Not that he will bless us with eternal benefits, but he already has. "He has seated us with him in the heavenly realms in Christ Jesus" (Ephesians 2:6). As followers of Christ, we are already living in the blessings of eternity—that is, heaven —while our feet still walk the earth.

Katie's lungs had less and less space available for breathing the air of earth because, spiritually speaking, her lungs were filling more and more with the air of heaven. She had been balancing the two realms for long enough, and eventually there just wasn't enough capacity for both. I think Katie would have loved to have experienced more of the joys of this world—I would have loved to have watched her do it—but if she had to choose, I also believe Katie would have said, "Give me Jesus."

In my mind, the image of Katie's last breaths on earth cannot be separated from her first breaths in heaven. I see her running, arms wide open, eyes wide open, lungs wide open breathing in the love of Jesus firsthand. Katie is where God wants her to be. And she is where she wants to be as well, because Jesus was the deepest desire of Katie's heart.

What Katie went through is no mistake. I will never understand exactly why this was the path her life went down, but it is a part of her story. Katie's story. And there is a greater purpose to Katie's story because of the perspective from which it was written. Not mine. Not hers. But God's. God wrote Katie's story from the perspective of eternity.

Let God's light shine in me.

Your light still shines, Katie. Your light still shines.

OAR concert with Josh and Betsy!!! :)

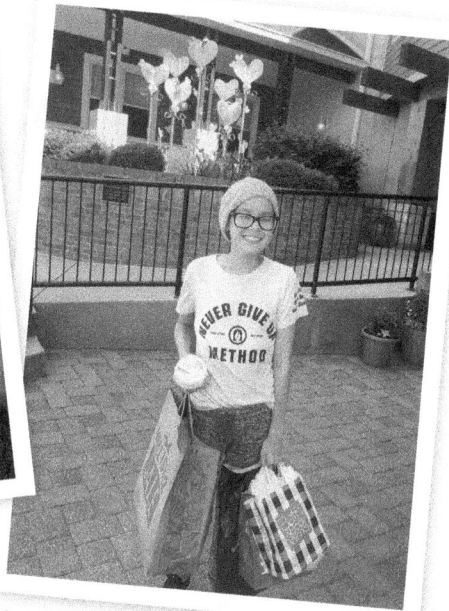

best way to spend an afternoon :))))

King's Island with the whole fam! love these crazy guys!

never grow up my little dood 🖤

if you don't go to taco bell and eat velveeta on sundays then you're not churching right :)

i love dogs so muchhhhh! :))

putt puttin' and soakin' up some rays :)))

lil' chunky babe 🖤

love them 🖤

i have the best friends. thank you everyone for celebrating #14 with me :)

there is beauty in simplicity 🖤

first day of high school!!! :)

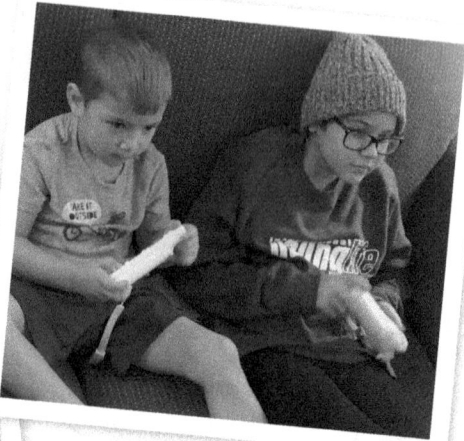

the Suite Life of Daniel and Katie

wicked with the padre 💜

if only i could eat this all the time!

best day ever

swimming with
dolphins!!!

because when you stop
and look around, this life
is pretty amazing

Cobb gals ♥

P.S.

Even though our mortal bodies will die, we can still have life. Katie would want you to know how much God loves you and wants to shine his light in and through your life. She wrote out a series of verses that can enable you to begin your own relationship with God through Jesus.

In order to claim to be a believer in Christ, we must have a basic understanding.

We were created to be in a relationship with God. But we messed that up (Romans 3:23).

The result of that mess up is death - eternal separation from God (Romans 6:23).

The good news is that Jesus came and died in our place (Romans 5:8).

If we accept Jesus, we can have a relationship with God again (Romans 10:9-10).

...for all have sinned and fall short of the glory of God...

— Romans 3:23

For the wages of sin is death, but the gift of God is eternal life in Christ Jesus our Lord.

— Romans 6:23

But God demonstrates his own love for us in this: While we were still sinners, Christ died for us.

— Romans 5:8

If you declare with your mouth, "Jesus is Lord," and believe in your heart that God raised him from the dead, you will be saved. For it is with your heart that you believe and are justified, and it is with your mouth that you profess your faith and are saved.

— Romans 10:9-10

About the Author

Sarah J. Cobb is the wife of one and mother of five. By day, she promotes health and wellness as a Family Nurse Practitioner. By night, she operates various pieces of heavy equipment, such as the dishwasher, stove and washing machine. If she could have any superpower, it would be to never need sleep. If calories didn't count, she would eat fresh bread and real butter for every meal. She is a pastor's wife and her husband's biggest fan, but she hates stereotypes, so she will warn you up front that she may not be what you expect her to be. However, she is okay with that and so is Jesus. They have already talked about it.

Sarah's passion is connecting women to women while simultaneously pointing them to Jesus, and she currently leads a ministry to women of all ages at River Ridge Church. In her pockets of time, she writes and blogs in hope that the things God reveals to her may somehow be helpful to others. Sarah is always excited to connect and share God's story with other women. Offer her a cup of tea or a power workout and she's there. She loves discipleship and small groups and is also available for large group speaking.

Follow Sarah's blog, Oaks of Righteousness, at www.sarahjcobb.com.

Facebook: sarah.j.cobb.9

Instagram: @sarahjcobb7

And listen to her as co-host of *MountainMovers* Podcast: https://mountainmovers.podbean.com

35th Star Publishing

www.35thstar.com

www.ingramcontent.com/pod-product-compliance
Lightning Source LLC
Chambersburg PA
CBHW062010090426

42811CB00005B/811